# From Savvy Saver to Smart Spender

*How to Pick a Tax-Wise Retirement*

*Withdrawal Strategy*

*2023 Update SECURE 2.0 Act*

Daniel W. McDonald

*From Savvy Saver to Smart Spender:*
*How to Pick a Tax-Wise Retirement Withdrawal Strategy*
*2023 Update SECURE 2.0 Act*

Daniel W. McDonald

© 2022, 2023 Daniel W. McDonald

Published by RTS Tech Publications LLC

ISBN: 979-8-88525-737-4 (Paperback Edition)
ISBN: 979-8-88525-738-1 (Ebook Edition)

*To my wife Kim*
*For supporting my dreams*

# Table of Contents

# Introduction

A re you in your fifties or sixties and about to retire or already retired? Do you expect your 401(k) and other accounts to total a few hundred thousand dollars or more by the time you start withdrawing from them? Then you are in the "sweet spot" for gaining maximum benefits from using the strategy outlined in this book.

Other books on finances in retirement focus on how to *save* your money for and enter retirement. But there is one big decision that these books ***don't*** help you make: How should you ***withdraw from your accounts*** to meet your monthly expenses in retirement? You spent decades accumulating savings to use in retirement. You put a lot of effort into how you *saved* that money. Shouldn't you put some effort into how to *spend* it wisely too?

Maybe you've wondered about this. I know I did. In my gut, I thought it could be an important and potentially costly decision. I was frustrated, however, by the lack of information and guidance on retirement withdrawals. (Could it be because the big financial institutions care a lot more about helping you *give* them money than helping you *take it out*? That's not for me to say.) Call it "withdrawal symptoms" with no cure.

Finding no answers to my questions, I decided to run the numbers myself by creating a retirement tax simulator I call the Retirement Tax Saver (created with the help of my son, a software engineer). The numbers showed that how and when money is withdrawn from tax-deferred and other accounts can have an enormous impact on taxes. I thought the information was important enough to share with others that I interrupted my attempt at early semi-retirement to write this book.

Maybe you have had "withdrawal symptoms" too. Maybe you haven't given it a second thought. Either way, this is a decision every retiree with substantial savings will make. For many, the decision will save—or cost—***thousands or even tens of thousands of dollars in taxes*** over the retirement years. Plus, with tax rates scheduled to increase in 2026, and potential tax increases even sooner, this decision is ***even more critical today***.

Some experts estimate that about 80 percent of retirees wait to use tax-deferred accounts such as 401(k) and IRA accounts until they "have" to withdraw from them at RMD age (when Required Minimum Distributions or "RMDs" begin—age 73 or 75 under the SECURE 2.0 Act passed in late 2022). While that "Conventional Wisdom" approach might save taxes pre-RMD age, it can wind up costing a lot *more* in taxes your mid-70s, 80s and beyond. This book shows you a better way that takes advantage of lower tax rates before you reach RMD age.

This book goes even further by helping guide you regarding *how much* you should withdraw before your RMD age to reduce your overall tax liabilities in the short or long run. Of course, every situation is different, including yours. How? This book sends you to a website where you can input your own account information into the Retirement Tax Saver tool and use a simple process to help you make this critical decision.

The Retirement Tax Saver can be tailored specifically to your situation—whether you are married filing jointly or single, when and how much you will receive in Social Security, your target income per year, and other information specific to you are all factored in. It even can help you estimate how much you can save compared to conventional, wait-to-withdraw wisdom. The Retirement Tax Saver will not calculate your exact future taxes owed—an impossible task, really. However, it *will* run simulations that will help you pick your best approach to withdrawals. And at least give you an idea of **how much** you may be able to save in taxes! The Retirement Tax Saver illustrates how wisely using low tax brackets pre-RMD age can help you avoid higher taxes in later years.

Finally, the book will walk you through how to **implement** the strategy you pick and how to **maintain** your strategy as your circumstances change in future years. You might be surprised to find that, even if it is late in the calendar year, you can still take steps to implement the strategy you choose **right now**. The strategy outlined in this book is so simple that you can implement its guidance and improve your future tax situation before this year is over.

Did I mention that this strategy does not require you to buy into any new insurance or investment products or pay a single cent in new fees, hidden or not, of any kind? This book is not trying to sell you any new products. It simply helps you withdraw your income needs from your *existing* accounts in a better way.

New in 2023: RMD age now varies from 73 for those born after 1949 to 75 for those born after 1958. https://www.msn.com/en-us/news/technology/retirement-new-rules-are-coming-for-401-k-and-ira-accounts-here-is-what-to-know/ar-AA15xy12. Whatever your RMD age, you could save big on taxes in retirement.

# Chapter One

## Don't Wait to Withdraw—How Implementing a Retirement Withdrawal Strategy Now Can Slash Your Tax Bill Later

*"Taxes are an often-overlooked aspect of retirement planning. . . . This is an important dynamic to understand and will prevent unnecessary surprises when you enter retirement."*[1]

Will you, or do you, receive enough in Social Security, pension income, and withdrawals from tax-deferred accounts to owe income taxes? Do you have any idea how much taxes will ravage your retirement savings? Before I started researching this book, I answered those questions for myself—or at least, I tried. The first one was easy. I had been working for more than thirty-five years and was excited to be able to consider retirement. I read a few financial books and magazines along the way, got a little investment help, and invested in 401(k), IRA, and regular accounts. I was sure I would owe taxes in retirement. Brilliant, eh?

But that second question? Not so much. Sure, I had accumulated financial knowledge that helped me invest for retirement (at least in my mind). I focused on *accumulating*

---

1   Larry Fox, "Consider taxes in your retirement savings strategy," *The (Waterloo, Iowa) Courier*, May 26, 2017, p. M14.

assets for retirement. Save, save, save. I was aware of income taxes, of course—I was reminded every paycheck, and again every April. While receiving a paycheck, I could move the tax-due needle based on payments to 401(k)s and a few deductions like charitable contributions and mortgage interest, but essentially my paycheck determined my tax bracket. I dislike jail as much as the next guy, so I duly paid my taxes.

### *Are You Ready for the Roller Coaster? A Successful Saving History Does Not Prepare You for a Successful Withdrawal Strategy*

As retirement neared, however, I found myself getting that queasy feeling when the roller coaster slows as it reaches the top of the hill. The savings years were like the ride up the roller coaster: so far, so good. Like that feeling on the roller coaster at its peak, however, as I neared retirement, I felt like the next part was going to be quite different, and nothing that happened before necessarily prepared me for what was next. It was unsettling—not in the physical way that a roller coaster ride is unsettling, but not that different either.

As I neared the peak of the "roller coaster," I thought I was ready for handling retirement finances. I had financial knowledge built over decades. In my fifties I read books and articles on retirement planning. By all means read whatever you can, but if you haven't read them yet, here is a Spoiler Alert: the general, unifying theme of all retirement literature is, *you need to save more*. OK, I will try.

Meanwhile, financial advisors and even websites of all sorts were happy to "run my numbers" and tell me how much money my wife and I could expect to have available each year in retirement. Or at least *project* how much money based on *projected* savings, *projected* investment returns, and *projected* dates of my spouse and me getting hit by a bus (buses?) or otherwise meeting our respective, and expected, demises. None of it seemed to be an exact science, but I thought the analysis was in the ballpark—or you could at least see the ballpark from there. I thought I had all the bases covered. What else can you do about the future?

*The One Thing Missing—Now Found*

Despite all the planning and reading, I realized, however, I was missing one thing. As I neared the date of retirement that one thing grew into a major source of that queasy, top-of-the-roller coaster feeling. That one thing was: ***how do I withdraw from my accounts to deal with taxes in retirement?*** I was not looking for a major overhaul of my accounts or investments. I just wanted to know how much I should take from each of my 401(k)s, IRAs, and other accounts that I already have to pay my expenses each year.

I dug a little deeper. Finding no books or articles on the subject, I dug out Congressional Research Service papers, IRS publications, and Center for Retirement Research analyses about retirement taxes. They talked about taxes in retirement, but they still did not answer the question.

As they say, nature abhors a vacuum. To fill the void, I wrote this book to answer the question and tell me and others like me the one thing I could not find anywhere else.

If you have, or expect to have, at least a few hundred thousand dollars in 401(k), IRA, and other accounts you will draw upon in retirement, congratulations. You are a Savvy Saver. However, you are likely to owe income taxes. It may not be at the same rate you paid when you were working, but it is still enough money to demand your attention. Sorry, but please don't shoot the messenger. Also, being good at saving money *in* those retirement accounts does not make you good at knowing what to do when you take the money back *out* of those accounts.

There is, however, potential good news on the tax front: unlike in your working years, in retirement you have **more control** over more decisions that can have a major impact on the taxes you owe because you have **new** levers relating to which accounts you withdraw your money from, and when.

I call that "potential" good news because, if you do not use the new levers correctly, the news isn't good at all. At best, it is a wasted opportunity. At worst, you will want to kick yourself because you had a chance to save money, but you ignored it. It is only good news if you use it.

How do the levers work? That is explained in the following chapters. The idea is that if you use the levers wrong (and in fact use them as some advisors suggest you should), you will pay more taxes than necessary. That is because the "conventional" approach often fails to make the best use of the lowest tax brackets throughout retirement.

How can that be, you may ask, if your plan is to use the same amount of money each year in retirement? Shouldn't the taxes be the same every year? Not necessarily. If you have multiple retirement accounts—including tax-deferred accounts as well as accounts which are not taxed as income when you withdraw the money from them—then your tax rate can vary widely depending on which account you use, when you use it, and how much you withdraw. The more you have saved in tax-deferred accounts for retirement, the more taxes you could owe—and the more you could save by making the right decisions.

That got my attention. But as I dug deeper, I realized that what I do in the earliest years of retirement— in other words, starting now—can have an outsized impact on taxes owed in retirement over the entire course of retirement. That is for two reasons.

The first reason relates to age. Call me a Younger Baby Boomer Saver. I am closer to the tail end of the baby boom, in my early sixties. Because I am retiring several years before I reach my RMD age, I have several years to take advantage of low tax rates to lower the balance in my 401(k) and IRA tax-deferred accounts in later years and lower taxes throughout retirement. That is good news, but it means I need to act now.

The second reason takes a little more explaining. Right now, federal income taxes are about as low as they have ever been. The highest current tax rate, 37 percent, compares favorably to the 39.6 percent and 50 percent top tax rates that were common in the years 1982-2017. You can thank the Tax Cut and Jobs Act of 2017 for that. Think of that law as a tax honeymoon.

The current rates will remain in effect—for now. As I write this book, the federal government is running record deficits that may lead Congress to raise taxes. That can change anytime Congress wants to change the law.

Even if Congress does nothing, however, on January 1, 2026, the honeymoon is over. Tax rates will rise to their higher, 2017 rates (adjusted for inflation). Not only will *rates* go up, but the *income levels* at which the tax rates change will kick in at *lower* levels of income. These changes will raise tax rates more dramatically for some people than others, depending on their taxable income.

In short, the second reason is that, if I take more money out of tax-deferred accounts *before* 2026, I will be able to make smaller taxable withdrawals *after* 2026. That is also good news but also requires me to act now.

Now that you know the story, let me cut to the chase. If you are near or in retirement but have not reached the age when RMDs begin, listen up. Your withdrawal strategy is important, and the easiest countermeasure you have available to deal with taxes in retirement, including the looming tax increases. This book gives you the skills and tools necessary to shift your thinking, understand the principles behind selecting a withdrawal strategy, and pick the best strategy for you. You will graduate from being a Savvy Saver to a Smart Spender.

As a Savvy Saver, you may have read several other books about investing, saving, and planning for retirement. That is good and should help make this book a lot easier to implement.

Many of those other books and resources give helpful guidance on what you should do *before* you retire. They are helpful in many ways about how to grow your assets and where to put them. But that's guidance about how to be a Savvy *Saver*—not necessarily a guide to being a Smart *Spender*.

For example, Charles Schwab Retirement Plan Center lists eight "Savings Fundamentals" but none relate to how you withdraw your money in retirement.[2]

Taxes sometimes seem to be treated like the outcast of the financial advice family—nobody wants to talk about them. "Although the notion of taking taxes into account when calculating retirement resources appears obvious, most empirical work on retirement decisions includes a value of retirement wealth before taxes. Moreover, only a handful of papers have addressed the impact of taxes on retirement income or wealth."[3]

The lack of discussion of taxes is not an indication that taxes are unimportant in retirement. To the contrary, according to *The (Cincinnati) Enquirer*, "Understanding which accounts to access and creating a withdrawal strategy is critical to maximize the longevity of your retirement savings and minimize your overall tax burden."[4]

---

2   Charles Schwab, "Fundamentals may help you grow savings over time," https://workplace.schwab.com/learning-center/eight-savings-fundamentals.

3   A. Chen and A. Munnell, "How Much Taxes Will Retirees Owe on Their Retirement Income?" Center for Retirement Research, November 2020, https://crr.bc.edu/wp-content/uploads/2020/11/wp_2020-16..pdf, at p. 7 .

4   Tom Cooney and Crystal Faulkner, "Retirement income is often taxable," The (Cincinnati) Enquirer Nov. 5, 2014, https://www.cincinnati.com/story/money/2014/11/05/retirement-income-often-taxable/18573995/.

Unfortunately, the lack of information leads to bad decisions. "Retirees...often fail to make adjustments that could lower their taxes."[5]

Other books may recommend strategies about how to invest your money for retirement. Some even suggest ways to move your money out of accounts that are taxed in retirement into new investments, insurance, or other devices that may be treated more favorably from a tax standpoint. Many of those options may involve additional costs, reduced returns, delayed benefits, or other features that make them either undesirable or unavailable for many people. They also may add complications that you just do not want to deal with. This book is not about purchasing new investment or insurance vehicles to replace your current accounts and holdings.

This book does not require, or even ask, you to buy new insurance or investment products. It works great with the accounts you already have. Much of the importance and relevance of the withdrawal decision comes from the fact that anyone with both a tax-deferred account and a "regular" account (or an "already-taxed" account, because if it is not tax-deferred, then it has already been taxed) is able to make the decision of which account to withdraw from in retirement. Millions of people are in that position, regardless of whether they made the moves other books recommend. Unlike many strategies that advocate or require certain types of investments, withdrawal strategy is based on a decision you need to make regardless of where you are invested. If your account holdings are like the cards in your hand in a poker game, whatever cards you currently hold in your hand, you need a strategy of how to play them. The right withdrawal strategy lets you play your hand in a better way.

If you are a Savvy Saver, you have a decent amount of money in accounts like 401(k)s and IRAs. While you were younger, the

---

5   Dave Carpenter, "Groundhog Day: 7 mistakes retirees make repeatedly," AP, Feb. 1, 2012, https://www.benefitspro.com/2012/02/01/groundhog-day-7-mistakes-retirees-make-repeatedly/?slreturn=20211106203741.

label "tax-deferred" on these accounts sounded great. Why pay taxes now if you can put them off until later? But as you near retirement, the day of reckoning draws nearer and nearer. When you retire, eventually you will withdraw money from these accounts. That money will be taxed as income on withdrawal. (This category is not meant to include Roth IRAs or Roth 401(k) s, which are "already taxed" and not subject to taxation on withdrawal.) While that day of reckoning is inevitable for most of us, a wise withdrawal strategy can help you save taxes once that day arrives, and thereafter.

Picking the right strategy, however, can be tricky. I doubt that I need to convince you that taxes are complicated, but as an example let's look at how the federal government taxes Social Security. Yes, Social Security *can be* taxed, although *how much* it is taxed requires calculation of something called "provisional income" equaling adjusted gross income plus certain tax-exempt income and half of Social Security benefits, *blah blah blah*.

By using a calculator to test various withdrawal strategies, we keep our focus on the strategy, not the math, and reduce the amount of uncertainty involved in the selection of a strategy. Uncertainty is reduced, but not eliminated, because there are countless numbers of ways individual accounts and situations can lead to different tax outcomes. The Retirement Tax Saver tool is not designed to calculate the exact amount of taxes you, me, or anyone else will owe even this year, let alone in any of the following ten, twenty, thirty or more years you will be needing retirement income.

What the calculator *does* do is allow us to test *and compare* various withdrawal strategies for hypothetical taxpayers with various account holdings to see which strategies minimize taxes in those scenarios. Then you can learn from that information and draw conclusions as to what strategy is best for you.

This book helps you manage taxes when you need to start withdrawing money in retirement. And it does so without forcing you to do a lot of math or understand every rule and exception to the rule regarding taxation in retirement.

I am sometimes accused of being a "numbers guy," so it was a labor of love for me to work with my son, a Computer Science graduate from Cornell University, to develop the Retirement Tax Saver engine.

## *Icing on the Cake: More Reasons the Right Withdrawal Strategy Will Save You Money*

There are other reasons why it could be valuable to select and implement a tax-efficient strategy. One is state income taxes. If you are in a state that taxes income, picking a withdrawal strategy can save you even more.

As shown above, Social Security may be subject to federal income taxes. If you are in a state that also taxes Social Security ("bad news" for those who would prefer to keep that income for themselves), the better news is that this book will help you even more. You may need it more than anyone. The following chart, taken from the Congressional Research Service's analysis of taxation of Social Security,[6] shows the states that 1) *exempt* Social Security from taxation, 2) do not tax *any* income including Social Security, 3) tax Social Security just like the feds (go Utah!) and 4) tax Social Security in a way *different* from the federal government:

## State Income Taxation of Social Security Benefits

*Thirty states do NOT tax Social Security benefits as income*:

---

6   Congressional Research Service, Social Security: Taxation of Benefits, RL32552, updated June 12, 2020, https://sgp.fas.org/crs/misc/RL32552.pdf.

Alabama, Arizona, Arkansas, California, Delaware, District of Columbia, Georgia, Hawaii, Idaho, Illinois, Indiana, Iowa, Kentucky, Louisiana, Maine, Maryland, Massachusetts, Michigan, Mississippi, New Hampshire, New Jersey, New York, North Carolina, Ohio, Oklahoma, Oregon, Pennsylvania, South Carolina, Tennessee, Virginia, West Virginia (new in 2022), Wisconsin

*Seven states do NOT have an income tax:*

Alaska, Florida, Nevada, South Dakota, Texas, Washington, Wyoming

*One state DOES tax Social Security and follows federal taxation of Social Security benefits:*

Utah

*Twelve states DO tax Social Security benefits in whole or in part but differently from federal taxation:*

Colorado, Connecticut, Kansas, Minnesota, Missouri, Montana, Nebraska, New Mexico, North Dakota, Rhode Island, Vermont

If you live in a state that taxes Social Security, this book will help you save even more.

Another reason the right withdrawal strategy is even more important right now has to do with coming increases in tax rates. A good withdrawal strategy can save you taxes even if tax rates stay the same forever. This is important because who knows what Congress will do or when they will do it. But if Congress does nothing (a real possibility if the past or present is any guide), tax rates are already scheduled to go up for most people in 2026.

In that event, the withdrawal decision could very well save you more. That is because the withdrawal strategies outlined in this book all result in shifting more of your taxable income into years before you must take Required Minimum Distributions (RMDs) from your tax-deferred accounts to avoid large penalties. It just so happens that for those people who will not be RMD age by 2026, such a strategy will also result in more income being taxed at pre-2026 rates, and less income being taxed in 2026 and thereafter. If you have less taxable income in the years in and after 2026, you have less income subject to these higher future rates. Common sense would indicate that a strategy which lowers your taxable income in future years will save you more in taxes in those future years if (and when) tax rates go up.

It is conceivable Congress will intervene to stop the increase. But who would want to bet on that happening? In any event, even if Congress does act, it will not hurt you. You just will not get this bonus benefit from making larger taxable withdrawals at the lower rates before tax rates increase.

The next chapter addresses several benefits of developing and implementing a tax withdrawal strategy. The remainder of the book will use the finances of several hypothetical retiring couples and singles to demonstrate the principles involved in developing a strategy, which for many will involve a shift in thinking as part of the transition from a pre-retirement Savvy Saver to a post-retirement Smart Spender.

You will identify the information you need to gather to make the decision and learn how to pick a better withdrawal strategy using the online Retirement Tax Saver. Finally, you will learn about additional benefits that can arise from picking a strategy, and how to implement and maintain the decision for the greatest tax savings over the duration of your retirement.

# Chapter Two

## Six Questions, Six Reasons You
## Need a Withdrawal Strategy

Are you in the top 20 percent of savers of assets for retirement? If so, congratulations. Worrying about how to withdraw from your retirement accounts is a much nicer problem to have than not having any retirement savings at all. But it means that you will be taxed in a significant way in retirement. And it means that choosing the right tax strategy could save you thousands or even tens of thousands of dollars in retirement.

Total asset value is just one component of the analysis. Several more factors come into play. Let's see how with six questions:

1) How much do you have, or will you have, in retirement assets?

2) What "Buckets" (types of accounts) do you have?

3) What other sources of income will you have in retirement?

4) How much do you expect to spend annually in retirement?

5) Does a financial advisor help you make financial decisions?

6) Are you already retired, or getting ready for retirement?

## Question 1: How much do you have, or will you have, in retirement assets?

The threshold for having "enough" assets to be significantly taxed may be lower than you think. According to the Center for Retirement Research (CRR) at Boston College, "[Tax] liability rests primary with the top quintile (top 20 percent) of the income distribution."[7] This includes millions of people who are in the top quintile of all U.S. taxpayers in terms of income. While people with lesser savings pay little or no taxes in retirement, these researchers found that "taxes, however, are meaningful for the top quintile."

"Meaningful" is a nice way, or maybe a researcher's way, to say "a lot." People who are in the top 20 percent probably have been paying more than "meaningful" income taxes most of their working lives.

Many of the people in that group may have assumed, or hoped anyway, that taxes might be less "meaningful" in their retirement years. The short answer is, not as much as one might think, if at all. The same CRR study determined that the top 20 percent pay an average tax rate on all retirement withdrawals of 11 percent (including 10.7 percent for married couples and 17.3 percent for single individuals). These rates may be lower than the rates applicable while working, but they are still significant—or rather, "meaningful." Plus, the marginal

---

7 Anqi Chen and Alicia H. Munnell, "How Much Taxes Will Retirees Owe on Their Retirement Income?" Center for Retirement Research, November 2020, https://crr.bc.edu/working-papers/how-much-taxes-will-retirees-owe-on-their-retirement-income/.

tax rate— the rate on the last dollar withdrawn—is likely to be much higher than 11 percent.

Are *you* in the top 20 percent? The CRR study's top 20 percent are mostly married couples with average IRA and 401(k) balances of $325,000 and total financial wealth of $441,400. Those numbers are (ahem) meaningful, but not necessarily eye-popping. According to the CRR study, "These households as a group are not what many would consider wealthy."

If you have or will have assets at or above these numbers, chances are your tax strategy can have a substantial effect on how much you pay in taxes during retirement.

Also, as you might expect, the more you have, the more important the withdrawal decision is. The tax rate for the top 5 percent jumps up to 16.4 percent of retirement income. They have average IRA/401(k) holdings of $497,500. The effective or overall tax rate goes up quite a bit—to 16 percent, up from 11 percent for the top 20 percent group as a whole—for not that much more in average assets. Moreover, if you thought the top 20 percent tax rates are skewed because they include the super-wealthy, think again. The CRR study notes that its survey population does not include the Bill Gates- and Warren Buffet-types.

Picking the right withdrawal strategy is obviously more important when you have more money. What may not be obvious is how little in assets it takes to become "meaningful," and how taxes in retirement can go up with relatively small increases in retirement assets. Surprisingly, sometimes the savings for couples with more modest accounts may actually be greater than the savings for some couples with larger accounts. If you have or will have any savings at all in retirement, you should look at taxes.

For someone with $1 million in retirement assets, the CRR study suggest that taxes will total over $150,000. Of course, that could vary widely based on the type of assets held and other factors. But the study suggests that for most people in the top 20 percent, the amount of money involved is nothing to sneeze at.

The bottom line is, if you are in the top 20 percent and have (or will have) more than about $400,000 in assets you are planning to use in retirement, there is a good chance the withdrawal strategy described in this book will help you save money.

### Question 2: What "Buckets" (types of accounts) do you have?

For most people, there are two main types of accounts or "Buckets" you can choose to withdraw from in retirement. It is important to know which buckets you have. The taxes owed for withdrawals can vary widely depending on how much you withdraw from each bucket.

The decision that affects how much in taxes you will owe: How much should you take out of each bucket? Obviously that question does not matter much if you don't have more than one bucket.

If your money is spread across multiple buckets, however, this book will help you decide how much to take out of each bucket each year to minimize your taxes. If you have many accounts, you may be especially motivated to simplify your withdrawal process with a systematic way to decide how much to withdraw from each account. Whether your assets come from two accounts or many, a withdrawal strategy can make a big difference.

Let's explain each bucket and how it may affect withdrawal strategy.

If you have most assets in **regular 401(k)s and IRAs (Bucket 1)**—you need to think carefully about withdrawal strategy because 100 percent of that money is taxable when withdrawn. By "regular" I mean it is not a Roth IRA or Roth 401(k).

Other tax-deferred accounts are taxed on withdrawal, too, such as annuities. One goal of this book is to keep things simple and not get buried in all the exceptions and related details. We will talk in terms of IRAs and 401(k)s, usually with a shorthand reference to both types of accounts as "401(k)" accounts, but annuities and some other accounts may well be appropriate for similar treatment.

The good news about these Bucket 1 accounts is that they saved you taxes in your pre-retirement years because the money you made in those earlier years to fund these accounts was not taxed when it went into these plans. Hooray for that.

The bad news is that Bucket 1 assets are not tax-free, they are only tax-*deferred*. That means at least some of the money, and maybe all of it, was not taxed like other income in the year you earned it. Instead, it is taxed later—when you withdraw it. Remember the old sayings, "The only things certain in this world are death and taxes" and "There is no such thing as a free lunch"? Well, there is a lot of truth in those old sayings for Bucket 1. Taxes are certain on Bucket 1 eventually, and the lunch bill is coming when the withdrawals start.

As I address in the next chapter and illustrate in Chapters 3-7, Required Minimum Distributions (RMDs) can create a huge tax bill in the years after RMDs begin. But with planning and action before your RMD age you can minimize or even eliminate this problem. People with significant assets in this Bucket (especially if they are not yet required to take RMDs) are among the people most likely to obtain tax benefits from careful consideration of a retirement withdrawal strategy.

Do you also have **non-IRA/401(k), already-taxed accounts such as a portfolio of mutual funds or stocks, or Roth IRAs/401(k)s (Bucket 2)**? The "bad" news and good news for Bucket 2 are the reverse of the good and bad news for the Bucket 1 accounts.

The government already collected taxes on those Bucket 2 accounts. For regular investment accounts, dividends, interest, and capital gains were taxed in the years they were generated. If the value of a stock or mutual fund goes up but it is not sold, the unrealized capital gains are not taxed. The gains are only taxed when they are "realized;" in other words, when the asset is sold. Otherwise, if it is a long-term account held for retirement, this account has probably been hit by taxes many times over many years.

The "good" news is that because (most) funds in these accounts have already been taxed, those dividends, interest, and previously-realized capital gains in Bucket 2 are not taxed *again* when the money is withdrawn. While Bucket 2 may still be subject to taxes on unrealized capital gains, in large part it has already been taxed and will be subject to little or no taxes when used in the future. In effect, you paid for lunch in advance. Lucky you—you do not have to pay for lunch again. Your taxes on withdrawals from Bucket 2 will typically be much lower than when you withdraw from Bucket 1.

If you do not have significant assets in Bucket 2, then there is not much this bucket can do for you from a tax-saving perspective. But if you do have significant assets in Bucket 2, that should provide the flexibility in withdrawal scenarios that you can use to implement a sound, tax-wise withdrawal strategy.

Withdrawals from Roth accounts are tax-free. These are beneficial accounts in retirement because nothing is taxed on withdrawal—interest, income, dividends, and even realized capital gains all can accumulate, but are never taxed. If Roth accounts are your only asset, you may think you do not need any help with tax strategy. But most people are not that lucky. "Roughly 10 percent of assets are held in Roth IRAs or Roth 401(k)s."[8]

Roth accounts are generally available only to account holders whose income is under the limit for adjusted gross income. In 2023 a married couple filing jointly cannot make

---

8 Anqi Chen and Alicia H. Munnell, "How Much Taxes Will Retirees Owe on Their Retirement Income?" Center for Retirement Research, November 2020, https://crr.bc.edu/working-papers/how-much-taxes-will-retirees-owe-on-their-retirement-income/, at 5.

contributions if their income is over $218,000.[9] The limit phases out at incomes between $218,000 and $228,00. However, there is an exception: people over the income limit can deposit after-tax money in a regular IRA and then immediately convert it to a Roth IRA without incurring tax liability resulting from the conversion. That is called a back-door Roth IRA. Also, you can convert regular IRAs into Roth IRAs if you are willing to pay taxes on the amount converted in the year of conversion.

The "no free lunch" rule comes into play for Roth accounts because the money as deposited into a Roth account is not tax-sheltered or tax-deferred. You must pay taxes on that money in the year you earn it or the year you convert the regular IRA or 401(k) account into a Roth account. Roth accounts are arguably the best accounts to have in retirement. They can help implement a strategy that minimizes the taxes owed.

Because Roth accounts and already-taxed money can all be withdrawn tax-free, we will combine these assets into Bucket 2. This keeps the analysis simple while still recognizing the fundamental difference between Bucket 1 assets (taxed when withdrawn) and Bucket 2 assets (not taxed when withdrawn, except capital gains realized on already-taxed accounts). However, we will on occasion mention situations where Roth accounts may be particularly beneficial.

The bottom line:

*If you have substantial assets in each of Bucket 1 and Bucket 2, then how and when you withdraw from each bucket is an important choice, and one that can save or cost you thousands of dollars in taxes.*

---

9   It's Official: Roth IRA Income Limits Have Increased for 2023, https://www.fool.com/retirement/2022/10/27/its-official-roth-ira-income-ranges-increased-2023/.

### Question 3: What other sources of income will you have in retirement?

Withdrawal strategy can also be affected by whether your combination of income sources includes not just the Buckets discussed for Question 2, but also additional income sources. Here are a few of the most common sources of other income.

**Social Security.** You may think that Social Security is not taxed. You would only be partially right. Social Security will be taxed federally if you have substantial taxable income from other sources. The threshold is not that high—people who benefit from this book will probably be taxed on Social Security. Some states tax it too. If you are in the upper 20 percent of savers, there is a particularly good chance you will have enough income during many years in retirement to trigger the tax on Social Security income.

Again, the CRR helps us get an idea of how much money this is for our top-20 percent group: They say the top quintile averages Social Security benefits of $50,882/year.

It may seem strange that a government-funded pension is taxed. It is not clear that was the original expectation, but times change. As incomes have risen, "the percentage of households owing taxes [on Social Security] increased sharply. By 2010, 47 percent of beneficiary households paid some taxes on their benefits, rising to about 55 percent today, and this share is ultimately projected to level off at 58% around 2030."[9]

For example, if you are married filing jointly with $40,000 in Social Security and $30,000 in other income counted in the provisional income formula, then your provisional income is one-half of $40,000, or $20,000, plus $30,000, for a total of $50,000. The IRS formula requires you to calculate two more numbers using 85 percent because provisional income exceeds

$44,000.[10] First, calculate 85 percent of Social Security, which equals $34,000. Second, calculate 85 percent of the amount, if any, that provisional income exceeds $44,000. Here that totals $6,000 ($50,000 minus $44,000) times 85 percent, or $5,100. Then add $6,000 for a total of $11,100. In this example, the taxable portion of Social Security totals $11,100, which is the lesser of the first number ($34,000) and the second number ($11,100). The upper limit on the percentage of Social Security that can be taxed is 85 percent. If you had $40,000 in Social Security benefits and $20,000 in other income, your provisional income would total $20,000 + $20,000 or $40,000. The taxable portion of Social Security is $4,000. Why? Because provisional income is between $32,000 and $44,000, you would pick the lesser of (1) 50 percent of your Social Security benefits (here, $20,000) and (2) 50 percent of the amount, if any, that provisional income exceeds $32,000 (here, 50 percent of $8,000, or $4,000).

Retirement withdrawal tax strategy can help lower taxes due on Social Security. It might even provide some guidance on when to start receiving Social Security payments—more on that later.

**Defined-Benefit Pension.** This is a pension that pays a fixed amount per month. Payments are usually fully taxable in the year of distribution. Only about 8 percent of workers aged 40-59 have a defined benefit plan; the percentage is slightly lower for younger workers.[11] Again, the top 20 percent may be in a different position: according to the CRR as of 2018, the top 20 percent get $25,879 each year in pension income, on average.

---

10   Provisional income is explained in more detail in Chapter Four. The explanation of the $44,000 threshold and other thresholds can be found at Social Security Administration, "Program Provisions and SSA Administrative Data," 2019, Table 2.A31, https://www.ssa.gov/policy/docs/statcomps/supplement/2019/2a29-2a32.html.

11   Center for Retirement Research, "Data," https://crr.bc.edu/data/.

Unlike Social Security, which is never fully taxed as previously explained, all your pension income is taxed like most other forms of income.

You probably do not have control over how big your pension check is every month, or when you start receiving it, even assuming you are lucky enough to qualify for one. However, tax strategy can guide what to do with the buckets in view of your pension income, and potentially lower the effective tax rate on that income.

**Annuities.** Annuities are financial products that involve up-front payments in exchange for future payments. They take many forms. Annuities are taxed on withdrawal, unless after-tax money is used to purchase them, which is withdrawn tax-free. If an annuity is paid for with tax-deferred dollars from a 401(k) or IRA, the entire distributions will be taxed.[12] This is another example of how the tax system ensures that virtually every dollar is subject to taxation eventually. For purposes of this book, we will simplify the analysis by treating 100 percent of annuity distributions as taxable.

**Working.** Working part-time or other forms of income is typically taxable income and thus can also move you into higher tax brackets. Tax strategy can help keep more of what you earn.

For purposes of our analysis, we will combine all these alternative sources of income together separately from Buckets 1 and 2. Why? Because while it is taxed like Bucket 1 when received, you may not have control over how much you receive from these sources—you get what you get. In contrast, you have some control over how much you withdraw from Buckets 1 and 2. The differences between these sources and our two buckets are important to our analysis, so we need to separate them.

Bottom line:

---

12  Kimberly Lankford, "How Annuities Are Taxed," Kiplinger, Mar. 8, 2013, https://www.kiplinger.com/article/insurance/t003-c001-s001-how-annuities-are-taxed.html.

*These other income sources are like those in Bucket 1 because they are taxed when received in retirement. Unlike our buckets, however, there can be less control over the amount received each year from these other sources. Having these additional sources of income is a good thing but will raise your taxes. If you have additional sources of income, you may also benefit from using the strategies in this book.*

### Question 4: How much do you expect to spend annually in retirement?

This is one of the most important questions to consider when you are planning for retirement: How much can you spend in retirement without needing to reduce your standard of living in later years?

Other resources are available to calculate this. One popular method is to use the "4% Rule" as a measure of how much you can withdraw from your retirement accounts.[13]

For example, if Bob and Mary have $1.25 million in retirement assets and all of it is in a regular IRA (Bucket 1), then 4 percent would be $50,000. In their first year, they would withdraw $50,000, and (maybe) adjust it for inflation in future years.

Let's assume Bob and Mary have other sources of income, such as Social Security (let's use $55,000) and pension income (let's use $40,000). In year one, they would have retirement income of 4 percent or $50,000 from retirement accounts + $40,000 in pensions + $55,000 in Social Security = $145,000/year. Fans of the 4% Rule would say that is a good estimate of how much Bob and Mary can take in each year. However, that

---

13  Investopedia, "Four Percent Rule," https://www.investopedia.com/terms/f/four-percent-rule.asp.

doesn't mean they will have $145,000 to spend, because they will need to pay taxes on almost all of that $145,000.

How much you can withdraw can be affected by how many years you expect to live in retirement. For most of us that is just a guess. As a benchmark, the CRR estimates that a 65-year-old man will have about twenty years in retirement. In other words, odds are you will live until about 85. The Tax Saver calculator runs the numbers to age 90.

However you want to calculate it, pick a number for your target annual income. This will give us an idea of your marginal tax rate during retirement. The marginal rate is the tax rate on the last or next dollar of income. It is also necessary to provide a target income amount to use the Tax Saver tool. It turns out that the Tax Saver tends to work well for target incomes based on the 4% Rule, but feel free to try other target incomes.

We will use tax brackets throughout the book because they are important. However, to get an idea of how much money per year in taxes we are talking about for Bob and Mary right now, we will use tax brackets and tax rates in effect for 2023 (as used throughout the book unless otherwise noted). Recognizing that any and all tax brackets and rates can change whenever Congress decides to do it (and the President signs off), Bob and Mary pay as follows:

For the part of Bob and Mary's taxable income up to the standard deduction ($27,700 if they are under 65, or $30,700 if they are over 65), they owe no taxes.

- For the portion of Bob and Mary's taxable income between $30,700 and $52,700, they pay the marginal tax rate of 10 percent, or $2,200.

- For the portion of Bob and Mary's taxable income per year between $52,700 and $120,150, they pay the marginal rate of 12 percent, for a total of $8,094.

- For the portion of Bob and Mary's taxable income above $120,150 (and because total taxable income is $145,000, which is less than the upper end of this tax bracket), they pay the marginal rate of 22 percent—almost double the prior rate—which applies to the excess ($24,850) for a total of $5,467 (Social Security assumed all taxable).

Total taxes are $16,571 for Bob and Mary ($0 + $2,200 + $8,094 + $5,467). Their overall tax rate is about 11 percent of their $145,000 in total income. The last dollar, however, is taxed at 22 percent. In other words, because their income was more than $120,150, each dollar over that amount is taxed at 22 percent, not 10 percent.

What if you could arrange withdrawals so that the income taxed at 22 percent could be taxed at 12 percent instead? That would save them at least $2,485 ($24,850 taxed at 22 percent versus at 12 percent, the next lowest bracket) per year. Could they lower the tax rate even further—to 10 percent or 0 percent—on that withdrawal? Those what-if questions have a lot to do with how to identify alternative withdrawal strategies that can save money.

All these figures are just for federal taxes. If you are taxed at the state level, the rates are typically lower and may be at different breaks in income levels. The Tax Saver tool only calculates federal taxes, but many states follow the same overall structure as federal taxes, starting with no taxes on income below a standard deduction and using higher marginal tax rates as income goes up. This may mean that lower federal taxes will also mean lower state income taxes—and at a minimum, a strategy that reduces federal taxes is unlikely to increase state taxes. Maybe we will deal with state taxes in a future book—but for now the focus stays on federal taxes.

Bottom line:

*If you have retirement savings of a few hundred thousand dollars or more, you will probably save at least $1,000 in taxes* *each year, and even more in many years by implementing the strategies of this book. As your expected retirement income rises, the savings will be even more as the tax rates rise to 24 percent, 32 percent, 35 percent, and 37 percent.*

*Bonus: If you are in a state with income taxes, a withdrawal strategy that lowers your federal taxes may also lower your state taxes—and at a minimum is unlikely to raise state taxes.*

### Question 5: Does a financial advisor help you make financial decisions?

If you make all your financial decisions on your own, obviously these strategies will help you.

If you made it this far into the book, you probably have accumulated more assets for retirement than most people. If so, good for you and congratulations. You earned the title of Savvy Saver.

If you get financial advice, ask yourself whether your advisor has ever explained, or even brought up, the issue of *how* you should withdraw your money in retirement for tax efficiency. If not, this book provides helpful information you are not getting anywhere else. At a minimum, this book gives you the information you need to ask your advisor the right questions to improve your withdrawal strategy.

"Even if you depend on professionals for your financial planning, I strongly urge you to educate yourself about personal finance. The more educated you are, and the more focused you will be on your investment objectives, the better you will be able to provide for your beneficiaries, and the more intelligent the discussions you will have with your financial planners and attorneys."[14]

If you get advice, and your advisor determines your withdrawals with taxes in mind, you may well be in great shape already. Even then, however, this book may help. It will tell you what questions to ask to make sure the advisor is doing the right thing.

Does your advisor have information about all the accounts you use or will use in retirement? You should double-check. They need to know all account balances to guide you on a retirement withdrawal strategy. Maybe you set up a new account and did not tell him or her. This might lead to a withdrawal strategy that is not optimal. This book will help you and your advisor pick the right strategy.

Bottom line:

*If you handle your finances yourself, this book gives you an easy guide to improving your tax situation in retirement. If, however, you have a financial advisor and already know they are implementing a thoughtful withdrawal strategy that 1) takes taxes into account over the short and long term and 2) is based on knowledge of all your buckets and income sources, this book will help you understand what your advisor is doing, and why. If you are somewhere in between—you have an advisor but are not sure what withdrawal strategy they are doing, or what information they have to make the withdrawal decision—this book will help facilitate a valuable conversation with your advisor that could save you money.*

---

14  Elliot Raphaelson, "A personal financial planning reading list," *Sarasota Herald-Tribune*, Feb. 25, 2017, https://www.heraldtribune.com/story/business/columns/2017/02/25/personal-financial-planning-reading-list/22077994007/.

## Question 6: Are you already retired, or getting close to retirement?

Understanding the effect of different withdrawal strategies on taxes in retirement is important for people in the years leading up to retirement, who have plenty of years left to implement a retirement withdrawal strategy. It is both important *and* urgent for those who have already retired but haven't reached the age of 72. Those pre-72 retirees may well be able to implement a withdrawal strategy that saves a fair amount of money, but for maximum benefit they can't wait long before the opportunity for savings will be lost.

Those who are in their late fifties to mid-sixties are in prime position to benefit from this point. Given that the baby boomer generation covers the birth years 1946-1965 or so, we are talking mostly about retirees at the end of the boom.

They are the Younger Baby Boomer Savers. And they have a chance to save a lot on taxes by selecting the right withdrawal strategy.

Plus, this group has a few years to go before they reach RMD age. That is important because at RMD age, retirees with 401(k) accounts are subject to heavy penalties if they fail to take the annual RMD from tax-deferred accounts. This requirement limits the withdrawal options and makes implementing a withdrawal strategy that saves taxes more difficult for those over RMD age.

If you are not yet retired and much younger than age 72, you have plenty of time to execute a smart withdrawal strategy, especially if you plan to have Bucket 1 and Bucket 2 balances by the time you retire. Also, such pre-retirees expecting to accumulate more assets between now and retirement may use this book to help decide how to allocate savings and investments between Bucket 1 and Bucket 2. You might not want to put all your retirement eggs in one bucket. Using both buckets can help provide more flexibility once a withdrawal strategy is implemented. For example, you might decide you want to put more money into a Roth IRA or a taxable account to give yourself more options to control taxes in retirement, even if that means paying more taxes before retirement than you would have paid otherwise.

Bottom line:

> *The Younger Baby Boomer Savers are in the best position to benefit from a wise withdrawal strategy because they have a few years before they hit RMD age. The more years until your RMD age that you have, the more options you have, and the more likely you will save money choosing the right strategy.*

The above six questions all show many reasons to consider and develop a tax-smart withdrawal strategy. Now let's talk about how to create that strategy.

# Chapter Three

## Moving From Savvy Saver to Smart Spender— Shifting Your Mindset on the Retirement Roller Coaster

*"One of the biggest retirement planning mistakes people make is not taking into account the taxes they will have to pay on their retirement income."*[15]

### Making the Transition from Savvy Saver to Savvy Spender: One Roller Coaster, Two Buckets

You may have spent years living below your means and making other smart financial decisions to have significantly more assets than most people. If so, congratulations on being a Savvy Saver. You probably have substantial assets in multiple accounts.

But those Savvy Saver days have ended or are soon drawing to a close. Now it is time to shift to being a Smart Spender. You are at the top of the Retirement Roller Coaster. You have finished, or nearly finished, the ride up the coaster—the work-and-save part of the ride. Now you are entering the ride down— the retire-and-spend part.

---

15   American Association of Individual Investors, "How Much of Your Retirement Income Will Go to Taxes?" AAII Journal, February 2021, https://www.aaii.com/journal/article/13439-how-much-of-your-retirement-income-will-go-to-taxes.

Like the parts of a ride on a roller coaster, these parts are very different. Having good Savvy Saver skills does not necessarily mean you have the Smart Spender skills necessary to efficiently withdraw your money in retirement, any more than the ride up the roller coaster prepares you for the ride down. The considerations are different in many ways, as the Quiz in Chapter Two might suggest.

Retirement is unlike a roller coaster in one key respect. You can ride a roller coaster over and over and learn what to expect at each point in the ride. For many people, they love riding the coaster over and over. Each time is more fun (at least for those people).

But when it comes to the shift from Savvy Saver to Smart Spender, everybody only gets to take the ride once. There is no practice run. We need to do what we can to prepare for the next phase as much as we can. We want to *pay* for lunch, not *lose* it, during the retire-and-spend phase.

Let's get to work preparing for the retire-and-spend phase. This requires a shift in thinking, just like you need to shift at the top of the roller coaster. To shift thinking, let's go back to basics, meaning back to buckets. Bucket 1, the bucket that you thought of as tax-friendly in your earnings years—regular 401(k)s and IRAs—now becomes your tax enemy. Conversely, Bucket 2 now becomes your friend. Other income sources such as Social Security may also help meet income needs but will be taxed and need to be factored into the strategy. All our strategies are based on the buckets. What are our options regarding how to use Buckets 1 and 2?

### Strategy A: Conventional Wisdom: The Wait-til-72+ Approach to Withdrawals

You might think the best strategy to minimize taxes is to delay using Bucket 1 as long as possible. In fact, some financial literature advises exactly that. For that reason, we will call this approach Conventional Wisdom. At first blush, that approach makes sense. If you owe taxes when you use Bucket 1 but owe little or no taxes in comparison when you use Bucket 2, then— duh—use Bucket 2. It's like the old joke where the guy goes to the doctor and says, "Doc, it hurts when I move my arm like this." The doctor's response? "Don't do that."

This approach defers taxable income until later years in retirement. In theory, you could have no taxable income at all in the early retirement years under this approach. The allure of this is understandable. After a lifetime of paying income taxes, you may be inclined to pop the champagne as your taxable income dives to levels lower than anything you've seen since you were much younger. Low taxable income means low taxes, which is great, right?

Well, sort of. There are (at least) two problems with that approach. First, you can't beat the system by putting off IRA and 401(k) (Bucket 1) withdrawals forever. When you reach RMD age, you must start withdrawing RMDs each year from regular IRAs and 401(k)s. You must, that is, unless you want to pay a whopping penalty (reduced to 25% from 50% in SECURE Act 2.0). When you start RMDs, 100 percent of the withdrawal is taxable as regular income when it is withdrawn. RMDs start at about 4 percent of the account balance for RMD-Age marrieds. The percentage gradually goes up with age. Check the sidebar to get more details about RMDs.

RMDs mean that, if you are lucky enough to make it to your mid-70s, the question is not *which* approach allows you to pay no taxes. You *will* owe taxes either way. The only questions are *when* and *how much* you owe.

Because RMDs don't kick in until age 72+, you may ask, can't you deal well with the taxes at least until you are 72 by withdrawing only from Bucket 2 until then? We can also more descriptively call this Conventional Wisdom approach the wait-til-72+ approach. Depending on how much you have in Bucket 2, and how many years you have before you reach 72, this may not be a viable option because you'll have to start using Bucket 1 before you reach 72 to meet your income requirements. But let's assume for a moment that you are in the enviable position of having enough in Bucket 2 that you could wait to withdraw from Bucket 1 until you reach RMD age. Doesn't the wait-til-72+ strategy for using Bucket 1 keep taxes to a minimum? Isn't that the smart way to go?

If you believe most of the Conventional Wisdom you read about retirement finances, you might be pretty sure the answer is "Yes." After all, many financial resources say that the right thing to do in retirement is to delay using the tax-deferred Bucket 1 dollars as long as possible. They say that this allows tax-deferred accounts to be invested and grow while delaying taxes on the gains. But for many retirees, this is the wrong answer, which leads to the second problem with the wait-til-72+ approach.

### The Plot Twist: Contrary to Conventional Wisdom, Taking Withdrawals from Bucket 1 before RMD Age Can Reduce Taxes over the Medium and Long Hauls.

From everything I had read, the wait-til-72+ approach to using Bucket 1 *appeared* to be the answer. Based on conversations I have had with many others in or near retirement, they thought (or assumed) the same thing. There is, however, something interesting about this advice: no one ever addressed the tax consequences of this strategy, let alone provided specifics regarding how much it would cost in taxes. I thought this was a warning sign to be careful about that approach and take a closer look.

As I dug deeper into the issue, however, I realized that **the Conventional Wisdom was wrong for me and thousands of others nearing retirement**. The surprising, counterintuitive answer to that question is that the wait-til-72+ approach can soak you with unnecessary taxes after you hit your RMD age. That's why I wrote this book.

38

The drawbacks with the wait-til-72+ approach to using Bucket 1 first require a little explaining relating to tax brackets.

Here is one of the areas where a change of thinking is in order as you transition from Savvy Saver to Smart Spender. You may have had the mindset during your Savvy Saver years that you couldn't do much about changing the tax bracket you were in. The goal was always to make as much income as you could, knowing you'd pay more in taxes because, even after taxes, the more you make, the more you keep. You could help yourself lower taxes by using exclusions and deductions like 401(k) and IRA contributions, mortgage interest, and charitable donations. Basically, however, you had no control over your bracket—taxable income was simply a foregone conclusion in view of your wage income.

But in retirement, your position changes. You have a great deal of newfound control over your taxable income on a year-to-year basis depending on whether you take money from Bucket 1 or Bucket 2. Withdrawals from Bucket 1 are taxable income, but withdrawals from Bucket 2 are not treated as taxable income.

That's power you never had during your earning years. Like Luke Skywalker (somewhat), now that you have the power, you need to understand how to **use** your power.

This power comes from the buckets and the brackets. We've already talked a fair amount about the buckets, so let's talk more about the brackets. Tax brackets give a break to people with lower incomes and take that break away from people with higher incomes. Apparently, Congress decided that the more money you make, the less of a break you need. The tax brackets provide some nice benefits at lower incomes.

Let's look at the tax brackets for 2023 as stated by the IRS:

For tax year 2022, the top tax rate remains 37% for individual single taxpayers with incomes greater than $578,125 ($693,750 for married couples filing jointly).

The other rates are:

35%, for incomes over $231,250 ($462,500 for married couples filing jointly);

32% for incomes over $182,100 ($364,200 for married couples filing jointly);

24% for incomes over $95,375 ($190,750 for married couples filing jointly);

22% for incomes over $44,725 ($89,450 for married couples filing jointly);

12% for incomes over $11,000 ($22,000 for married couples filing jointly).

The lowest rate is 10% for incomes of single individuals with incomes of $11,000 or less ($22,000 for married couples filing jointly).[16]

Those are the brackets as defined by the IRS. You probably don't remember the exact numbers off the top of your head, but you remember the concepts: generally, the more income you make, the higher rate you pay. No surprise there.

Let's add one more bracket: the 0% bracket. The IRS doesn't call it that, but in effect there is one. That's because everyone also gets to use a standard or itemized deduction to reduce the income that is subject to the brackets listed above. For married couples filing jointly (MFJ) who are under age 65, in 2022 the standard deduction is $27,700. For individuals it is half of that—$13,850. If you are over 65, the standard deduction rises

16 *IRS provides tax inflation adjustments for tax year 2023*, Internal Revenue Service, https://www.irs.gov/newsroom/irs-provides-tax-inflation-adjustments-for-tax-year-2023.

by $1,500 for MFJ and doubles to $3,000 if you are both over 65 for a total of $30,700. For single filers over age 65 the standard deduction increases $1,850 for a total of $15,700. That's enough money that it should not be ignored or cast aside lightly.

Below, this same information is translated to show the highlights for the brackets (using married filing jointly filing status as an example):

- **You will owe _no taxes_ on annual income up to your deduction** (the **$27,700** standard deduction is the minimum, or **$30,700** if you are a couple and both are over age 65). (Woo-hoo!)

- **You may owe _no taxes_ on an even higher amount** if you itemize and have a deduction higher than the standard deduction based on things like mortgage interest and charitable contributions. (Whoopee!)

- **You only owe 10 percent on the next $22,000 above the deduction.** (All right!)

- **You only owe 12 percent on the next $67,450.** (Cool!)

I add cheering at the end of each line because those are some fairly low tax rates that apply to at least your first $120,150 in income. (That number comes from adding up the $30,700 standard deduction plus the next two ranges noted above for the 10% and 12% brackets.) Taxes for a couple aged 65 or older owed on $120,150 of income total $0 on the first $30,700, $2,200 on the next $22,000, and $8,094 on the next $67,450 for a total of $10,294. That's about 9 percent of the total. Above $120,150, the tax rate jumps to 22% and goes up from there.

Note: the IRS's version of "taxable income" is determined as adjusted gross income minus the deduction taken, whether it is the standard deduction or itemized deductions. For a couple who has $25,000 in income, they would have $0 in "taxable income" the way the IRS looks at it. This book will use the term "taxable income" as comparable to the IRS definition of adjusted gross income, because we want to know income that does not exclude the deduction. For example, for a married couple filing jointly over 65 years old that actually has $32,000 in income that is subject to taxes, whether from a side job, a pension, or withdrawals from 401(k) accounts, this book calls that $32,000 in taxable income. The IRS definition, on the other hand, would say that couple only has $1,300 in "taxable income" because $32,000 minus their standard deduction of $30,700 equals just $1,300. Throughout this book, references to "taxable income" mean in the non-IRS sense, like adjustable gross income, before subtracting any deduction.

## Use it or Lose it

The ways the brackets are set up means that, even though the Bucket 1 withdrawals can in theory be taxed, up to at least $30,700 per year those **taxes will remain at $0** for the years leading up to 72 (assuming you have no other sources of income, which we will address later). Like the wait-til-72+ approach, there are no taxes owed before 72.

Suppose you have a year where you (and your spouse) have $0 in taxable income because you took nothing from a tax-deferred account. Then the next year you withdrew $60,000 from an IRA. In the first year, you have no taxes. In year 2, however, you will owe $0 on the first $30,700 of income, 10% or $2,200 on the next $22,000, and 12% or $876 on the last $7,300. Total tax: $3,076. If, on the other hand, you spread that same taxable income over two years, and took $30,000 each year, you owe zero taxes both years. Just like that, you save $3,076 in taxes on the same total withdrawals based just on the timing.

Think of the lower tax brackets as the equivalent of vacation days at a job. You might get four weeks of vacation every year. At many employers, you will lose some or all those vacation days if you fail to take them in the year they were awarded. Of course, people take all their vacation time every year because they don't want to lose it, right? Wrong. A recent study estimated that American workers did not use 705 million vacation days and forfeited 212 million vacation days.[17] In other words, even though they know they will lose vacation days if they don't use them, many workers lose vacation days every year.

"Use it or lose it" applies to the lowest tax brackets as well. The lower tax brackets are "use it or lose it" each year. In the example above if you take nothing the first year and $60,000 the second year, the IRS doesn't let you retroactively "spread out" your income to use the standard deduction you failed to use the prior year. You have to plan ahead. It's on you. Similarly, if you have no or low taxable income in the years leading up to RMD age because you elect to delay withdrawals from Bucket 1 as long as possible, then you lose the use of the lower brackets each year. You lose the benefit of the 0% rate for income up to $30,700 (or your itemized deduction if it is greater than $30,700), 10% on the next $22,000, and 12% on the next $67,450. Like lost vacation days, your chance to use those lower brackets in any given year is lost if it is not used that year, never to return.

## Buckets Bonus

Important: The situation turns more favorable for the years *after* 72 if you start withdrawing from tax-deferred accounts (Bucket 1) *before* 72. After 72, the taxable RMD drops because Bucket 1 is smaller. RMDs are determined based on (1) how

---

17   U.S. Travel Association, "State of American Vacation," 2018 (most recent available), https://www.ustravel.org/system/files/media_root/document/StateofAmericanVacation2018.pdf.

much money is in the account and (2) age. Less money in the account means a lower taxable RMD. RMDs in the following years will go down as well. Meanwhile, more non-taxable assets are left in Bucket 2, which is great because taxes are lower the more Bucket 2 is used.

Bonus: the standard deduction is indexed for inflation.[18] This adjustment occurs every year. That means this approach to earlier 401(k) withdrawals will reap more rewards in future years. For example, in 2022 the base standard deduction increased $800 to $25,900. Future increases will depend on actual inflation rates and will vary. It also means, however, that it would be useful to review your withdrawals annually to address any changes. This is just one reason to stress the importance of annual reviews.

### Debunking the Myth that Deferring Withdrawals from Tax-Deferred Accounts Always Makes More Money

Why do so many resources advocate for waiting to use tax-deferred accounts until every other account (except Roth IRAs and 401(k)s) is exhausted? They don't really explain. The theory seems to assume that tax-deferred accounts will grow bigger, faster. The assumption being that taxes in a tax-deferred account don't take a bite out of earnings in the years there are no withdrawals, which should leave bigger gains even after taxes are taken out on withdrawal in the future.

Does that assumption hold water? One thing you may notice is that the advocates for the waiting approach do not provide the numbers to support that approach. Once we run the numbers, we see that assuming that waiting to use deferred accounts will

---

18  Internal Revenue Service, "IRS provides tax inflation adjustments for tax year 2022," Nov. 10, 2021,  https://www.irs.gov/newsroom/irs-provides-tax-inflation-adjustments-for-tax-year-2022.

generate higher after-tax returns is a weak assumption at best, and wrong for many retirees.

The main reason waiting may not produce better after-tax returns is the unfavorable tax treatment of capital gains in tax-deferred accounts. When withdrawn, capital gains in tax-deferred accounts are taxed at the same rate and the same way as regular income, like dividends or interest.[19] In contrast, *capital gains in regular accounts are taxed at a rate lower than the income tax rate used to tax those gains in tax-deferred accounts*. This difference is most striking for couples with taxable incomes under $120,150 (or under $117,150 for couples under age 65). For these lower-income taxpayers, they pay *zero* on capital gains. A couple with taxable income below $120,150 but above $52,700, on the other hand, would pay a 12% marginal income tax rate.

Let's try an apples-to-apples comparison to illustrate the point. Jim and Jane have $100,000 in each of two accounts—a tax-deferred IRA and a regular account. Let's assume both accounts are invested in the same fund and grow 10 percent a year in the form of 2 percent dividends and interest and 8 percent capital appreciation. They need $20,000 each year for five years. They are deciding which account to use for those withdrawals, and which account to leave alone for five years. Which account will have more after-tax money in five years?

If tax rates were the same on all income in both scenarios, then leaving money in the tax-deferred account would be the clear winner (Conventional Wisdom). After five years that account will be worth the starting amount multiplied by (1 + 10%) five times, or $1.10^5$, which equals 1.61051. $100,000 * 1.61051 = $161,051 – an impressive increase of $61,051. If they are in a 12% tax bracket, they would owe taxes of $61,051 * 12% or $7,326. That leaves them with **$53,725** in net gains, after taxes.

---

19   H&R Block, "What are the taxes on a 401(k) distribution?" https://www.hrblock.com/tax-center/income/retirement-income/taxes-on-401k-distribution/.

On the other hand, if they leave the money in the regular account, it grows more slowly because taxes must be paid on income and capital gains every year. If we assume that *same 12%* income tax rate applies each year, then only 88 percent of appreciation is kept—yielding 8.8 percent after taxes each year on 10 percent growth. Multiplying the base amount ($100,000) by $(1.088)^5$ equals $152,456. This amount will not be taxed again, but even so this yields **$52,456**, which is $1,269 less than the after-tax amount taken from the tax-deferred account. *If the tax rates were actually the same*, which they are not, leaving money in the tax-deferred account would have been a smart way to go (although the difference is not dramatic after five years, totaling less than 3 percent of the amount of appreciation and about 1 percent of the starting amount).

Now let's use *real* tax rates. In recent years, most appreciation on mutual fund accounts owning stocks has been in the form of capital appreciation taxable as capital gains, not dividends and interest taxed as income. Capital gains are not taxed at all if taxable income is below $120,150. Even at higher amounts the capital gains tax rate is lower than the income tax rate as shown in this table (assuming a married couple aged 65+ filing jointly):[20]

| Taxable Income | Capital gains rate | Income tax rates |
|---|---|---|
| $0 - $120,150 | 0% | 0%, 10% , 12% |
| $120,150 - $584,550 | 15% | 12% - 35% |
| Above $584,550 | 20% | 35%, 37% |

---

20  Capital Gains Tax Rates for 2022 and 2023, https://www.forbes.com/advisor/taxes/capital-gains-tax.

Let's see what happens to Jim and Jane's taxes when we again assume 2 percent of the annual appreciation is dividends and interest and the other 8 percent is capital gains. If they leave money in the tax-deferred account, as before they would earn $61,051. If they are in a 12% income tax bracket, they would owe taxes of $61,051 * 12% or $7,326 as before. Remember— all gains are taxed as income in a tax-deferred account. That again leaves them with **$53,725** in net gains, after taxes.

If they used an after-tax account, in Year 1 they would earn 2 percent on their $100,000 or $2,000 in dividends and interest, taxed at 12%, leaving $1,760. The other 8 percent or $8,000 is capital gains and is *not taxed at all*—they are in the 12% *income* tax bracket but are in the 0% *capital gains* bracket. They keep all $8,000 in capital gains after taxes. After year 1, after taxes, their net gain is $9,760 or 9.76 percent. Applied over five years, this multiplies out to (1.0976)^5 or 1.593. Since they started with $100,000, they will end up with $159,300 after taxes. The after-tax gain, **$59,300**, is now *$5,675 more* than the after-tax gain in the tax-deferred account (about 10 percent more). The benefit of lower capital gains tax rates in a non-tax-deferred account causes the tax-deferred growth approach to lose its luster. Indeed, the advantage to the non-deferred account is more than four times bigger than the advantage to the tax-deferred account in the prior scenario where we assumed the tax rates are the same. The idea of locking up the money in tax-deferred accounts for an additional five years does not look like such a great option anymore, does it?

Which approach is better, and by how much, will vary by the actual appreciation rate, number of years involved, and other factors. For example, if more years of deferral are involved, the relative performance of tax-deferred accounts improves. But at a broad level it is fair to conclude that tax-deferred growth is not all it is cracked up to be when capital gains are a significant portion of the growth in account value. That is especially true for our analysis, which focuses on early

401(k)/IRA withdrawals for the years immediately after retirement and before RMD age. This is a relatively short period of time—perhaps five to ten years for most people—so the benefit of allowing a tax-deferred account to grow for much longer periods, such as twenty or thirty years or more, does not apply.

You could invest the money solely in bonds or interest-bearing accounts, which will have only interest taxable as income and no capital gains. You would avoid paying income tax rates on capital gains. That might be winning a tax battle but losing the investment war. In recent years the return on bonds has been very low.[21] At those returns, the benefits of tax deferral are negligible, amounting to about a tenth of a percentage point (about 4.6 percent in total after-tax return vs. 4.5 percent after taxes in a regular account) over five years at a 1 percent annual interest rate, for example.

The tax calculator does not calculate taxes at capital gains rates. Capital gains can and do vary widely (or even become losses) from year to year, making such a computation of limited value. The above analysis, however, shows that the calculator nevertheless provides a useful comparison of various withdrawal rates. That is because there is little to no loss of account growth when withdrawals are taken from tax-deferred accounts earlier than required. Those supposed benefits of tax-deferred compounding are negligible or do not exist for the number of years involved and for accounts which rely more on capital gains for appreciation than dividends or interest.

---

21  U.S. Department of the Treasury, "Resource Center," https://www.treasury.gov/resource-center/data-chart-center/interest-rates/pages/textview.aspx?data=yield.

## *The Biggest Beneficiaries of the Buckets Bonus: Younger Baby Boomer Savers*

The discussion above shows that we might want to proactively withdraw money from Bucket 1 in the years *before* RMD age, which is when we *have* to start withdrawing money from Bucket 1, to ensure we "use" and don't "lose" the benefits of the lower tax brackets. There are limitations on this approach, however. For example, if you are already 72 years old, you don't have the opportunity to change your withdrawal approach pre-72 (unless you are Marty McFly, which is a reference you should know if you are over 72).

For whom does this approach work? Recall from Chapter Two that we introduced the group we called the Younger Baby Boomer Savers. These are people in their mid-fifties to late-sixties who have or will retire, or at least start withdrawing money from their retirement accounts, well before age 72, but also after age 59 ½ to avoid penalties (although earlier penalty-free withdrawals are allowed under some situations). These Younger Baby Boomer Savers are the in the best position to maximize the benefits of taking voluntary withdrawals from Bucket 1 before RMDs become mandatory for them. That is why, if you fit in this group, you are in the "sweet spot" for the approaches described in this book.

So that's all well and good, but what then do we do? We will find out when we meet Roy and Tami in the next chapter.

# Chapter Four

## Let's Get Specific—How a Couple with Retirement Accounts Totaling $1.2 Million Can Simply Save Almost $20,000 in Taxes with a Smart Withdrawal Strategy

Let's introduce a hypothetical couple, Roy and Tami. They have $900,000 in an IRA (Bucket 1) and $300,000 in a regular account (Bucket 2). This is more than the average for a couple in the top 20 percent of savers, but in the ballpark of retirement savings for millions of people. They are 65 years old. They want $40,000 in income each year. To simplify the comparison of options, assume they have no Social Security or other income, and their accounts do not grow over inflation.

### Roy and Tami 1.0 (Simple example)

| | |
|---|---|
| **Bucket 1 (401(k)/IRA) account balance at retirement:** | **$900,000** |
| **Bucket 2 (already taxed) account balance at retirement:** | **$400,000** |
| **Retirement Ages: 65** | |
| **Target annual income:** | **$40,000/year** |

Now Roy and Tami have a decision: How much money should they withdraw from each of Bucket 1 and Bucket 2 to reach their target annual income of $40,000 (plus any income taxes they may owe)?

### Strategy A: Wait until RMDs Begin at Age 75 before Withdrawing from Traditional IRA and 401(k) Tax-deferred Accounts (Conventional Wisdom)

One approach is what we will call Strategy A (Conventional Wisdom). This approach means you wait to use the tax-deferred money in Bucket 1 as long as you can without incurring penalties. In other words, don't use Bucket 1 until Required Minimum Distributions (RMDs) are due at 75 (their RMD age).

If you assumed you would use Strategy A, you are not alone. The CRR cites a study based on IRS data as showing that only 20 percent of IRA and 401(k) account holders withdrew funds from those accounts before RMDs kick in—which means that 80 percent used Strategy A.[22]

Strategy A provides instant gratification. You avoid income taxes in the early years when withdrawing only from Bucket 2 (assuming that you are younger than 73). While the Center for Retirement Research 2020 analysis of taxes did not analyze the possible approaches to withdrawals, it assumes this approach.[23] Strategy A allows Bucket 1 to grow tax-deferred for more years, which is the apparent reason some literature recommends it "generally": "As a general rule, tapping taxable accounts

22   A. Chen and A. Munnell, "How Much Taxes Will Retirees Owe on Their Retirement Income?" Center for Retirement Research, November 2020, https://crr.bc.edu/wp-content/uploads/2020/11/wp_2020-16..pdf, at 6, citing Jacob A. Mortenson, Heidi R. Schramm, and Andrew Whitten, "The Effects of Required Minimum Distribution Rules on Withdrawals from Traditional IRAs," National Tax Journal 72(3): 507-542, September 2019.

23   *Id.* at 11.

first makes the most sense. This allows you to maximize tax-deferred growth in your qualified accounts."[24] "Generally, it's a best practice to allow money with more favorable tax treatment to stay invested for as long as possible..."[25]

What does it mean to defer withdrawals from Bucket 1 as long as possible with Strategy A? It means you wait until RMDs are required. In theory you could wait even longer, but then you'd pay a huge penalty (50 percent of the required amount not withdrawn) if you don't withdraw at least the RMD. Strategy A assumes you delay until RMD age, which is the latest you can start withdrawals without paying that penalty, and that you withdraw at least the RMD to avoid a penalty.

If Roy and Tami use Conventional Wisdom (Strategy A) and wait to use Bucket 1 as long as possible, then they would withdraw $40,000 from Bucket 2 each year from 65 to 74— a total of ten years. That's $400,000 of already-taxed withdrawals over ten years, leaving nothing in that account. No taxes owed. So far so good.

But at 75, that changes. Bucket 2 is empty, so Roy and Tami must withdraw the entire $40,000 from Bucket 1. The RMD is $36,585 ($900,000 divided by 24.6, their RMD divisor). They withdraw slightly more to meet their income needs of $40,000. Federal income taxes will be $1,033 on the $40,000 (plus taxes) withdrawal. For this and all other scenarios used in this book, taxes are paid from the already-taxed account unless that account reaches a $0 balance, at which point the 401(k) account is used (which itself results in additional taxes being owed). Because Roy and Tami have nothing left in their already-taxed Bucket 2 account, the additional $1,033 comes from Bucket 1. (Note: Your first RMD withdrawal is due by April 1 of the year following the year you turn RMD age, but to

---

24  Tom Cooney and Crystal Faulkner, "Retirement income is often taxable."

25  Larry Fox, "Consider taxes in your retirement savings strategy."

keep things simple we will treat the withdrawal as happening the year they turn 75.)

Here's the snapshot of this Conventional Wisdom, Strategy A scenario:

### Strategy A: Conventional Wisdom Approach (Wait to withdraw from Bucket 1 until RMDs are required or Bucket 2 runs out)

### Roy and Tami 1.0

Bucket 1 assets at age 75 (beginning of year): $900,000
Bucket 2 assets at 75 (beginning of year): $0
Bucket 1 withdrawal at 75: $40,000
Bucket 2 withdrawal at 75: $0

**Taxes owed 65-74: $0**
**Taxes owed at 75: $930**

Withdrawals from Bucket 1 will equal the RMD due plus any additional income needed to reach the $40,000 annual income target. Bucket 2 runs out of money by age 75. In the years after that, Bucket 1 base withdrawals (not counting taxes owed) will be the greater of (1) the RMD and (2) $40,000, the target income. Both the base withdrawals and the withdrawals needed to cover taxes are taxed when they come from Bucket 1.

When we run the numbers for future years with our Retirement Tax Saver tax estimator (more on that later), we find the total estimated tax burden adds up as follows:

## Strategy A:Conventional Wisdom Approach

### Roy and Tami 1.0

| | |
|---|---|
| **Total cumulative taxes owed through age 80:** | **$6,200** |
| **Total cumulative taxes owed through age 90:** | **$16,533** |

Is there a better withdrawal strategy? (Hint: I wouldn't have written this book if there wasn't).

### *Introducing Strategy B: Don't Wait to Withdraw*

Now let's have Roy and Tami try an approach that involves withdrawing a fixed amount annually from Bucket 1 starting at 65, when they retire, instead of waiting until age 75. We will call this Strategy B. This will save more of Bucket 2 for later when they need to take taxable RMDs from Bucket 1. It should also reduce the RMD amount, since Bucket 1 will be smaller and RMDs are based on the value of Bucket 1.

This approach gives Roy and Tami taxable income in pre-75 years. But that doesn't mean they have to *pay* taxes on that income. Remember, the taxable income up to the standard deduction, $30,700 for a married couple age 65, effectively is taxed at 0%. If the withdrawals are done in a way that takes full advantage of the 0% (standard deduction), Roy and Tami can withdraw a fair amount of taxable income from Bucket 1 while paying no taxes by 75 and reduce the RMDs owed after 75. This contrasts with Strategy A, which can "potentially push you into a higher tax bracket" through higher RMDs.[26] Strategy B gives Roy and Tami, and you, a chance to pay lower taxes in post-75 years, with little or no additional taxes owed in pre-75 years.

Some experts have recognized the problem with Strategy A. "A plan of gradual withdrawals [from IRAs and 401(k)s] starting in your 60s can be a more effective strategy" than "[p]utting off taking withdrawals from an IRA until they are required."[27] However, there is little guidance on how an alternative to Strategy A would actually work. After running a variety of scenarios using my Retirement Tax Saver tool, I am pleased to report that Strategy B *does* work better than Strategy A for Roy and Tami, when the right withdrawal amount is selected.

For Strategy B, let's assume Roy and Tami decide to withdraw the amount of the standard deduction for a couple aged 65, $30,700, from their Bucket 1 IRA/401(k) accounts each year until age 75. At 75, they will switch to RMDs. $30,700 is a number worth testing because we know they will not be taxed on income up to this amount. They make up the remaining income needed, $9,300, from Bucket 2. By RMD age of 75 they won't owe any taxes because their taxable Bucket 1 withdrawal never exceeds the $30,700 standard deduction. Bucket 2 goes from $0 under Strategy A to $307,000 under Strategy B at age 75.

Here is Roy and Tami's snapshot at 75 using Strategy B with a $30,700 annual withdrawal from Bucket 1:

---

26 Windgate Wealth Management, "Reflections: Which Accounts You Should Draw Down First in Retirement?" https://windgatewealth.com/which-accounts-should-you-draw-down-first-in-retirement/.

27 Dave Carpenter, "Groundhog Day: 7 mistakes retirees make repeatedly," AP, Feb. 1, 2012, https://www.benefitspro.com/2012/02/01/groundhog-day-7-mistakes-retirees-make-repeatedly/?slreturn=20211106203741.

## Strategy B: The Targeted Bucket 1-Withdrawals Approach (Targeting $30,700 in Bucket 1 withdrawals from age 65 to 75)

### Roy and Tami 1.0

Bucket 1 assets at age 75 (beginning of year): $593,000
Bucket 2 assets at 75 (beginning of year): $307,000
RMD (Bucket 1) at 75: $24,106
Bucket 2 withdrawal at 75: $15,894

**Taxes owed at 65-71: $0**
**Taxes owed at 75: $0**
**Taxes saved at 75 vs. Strategy A: $1,033**

Savings arise right away at age 75 to the tune of $1,033. The RMD dropped from $36,585 to $24,106. Because the already-taxed account has money left in it, we use that account to make up the difference ($15,894) to get to $40,000.

Key from a tax standpoint, Roy and Tami's standard deduction is $30,700 (using 2022 tax tables). That means *none of the Bucket 1 withdrawal is taxed using Strategy B when RMDs begin*, because the Bucket 1 withdrawal stays under $30,700 after 75 years of age. In contrast, using Strategy A, the Bucket 1 withdrawal is $41,033 to cover the needed income and taxes. The higher withdrawal creates $10,333 in additional taxable income that is taxed in Strategy A at 10%, leading to the $1,033 tax payment due when the first RMD is withdrawn. Roy and Tami **save $1,033 in taxes at age 75.** That's after paying no taxes between 65 and 75, just like the Strategy A: Conventional Wisdom strategy of deferring Bucket 1 withdrawals until RMDs are due. The entire $1,033 per year is *pure savings*.

Now let's get more good news about Strategy B.

What happens to Roy and Tami's taxes owed *after* 75? They *continue to be lower using Strategy B*—in fact, they **disappear!** That is because the Bucket 1 assets at age 75 that are taxed on withdrawal dropped in value by $307,000—from $900,000 using Strategy A to $593,000 using Strategy B. Meanwhile, the already-taxed Bucket 2 account balance at 75 increases from $0 in Strategy A to $307,000, a corresponding increase in available money that will not be taxed on withdrawal in the future. That additional Bucket 2 money also can be used to pay taxes in future years, without incurring additional tax liability on the additional withdrawal as would happen if Roy and Tami used Bucket 1 for taxes.

The lower Bucket 1 balance and higher Bucket 2 balance at age 75 allows for lower taxable distributions in future years. RMDs are determined by dividing the Bucket 1 account value by the IRS divisor, so the lower the account value, the lower the RMD. And as long as Bucket 2 can make up the difference to get to the target income amount, taxes will stay lower or even be eliminated.

Agreed, $930 in savings isn't huge. But that's just one year. Over the course of Roy and Tami's retirement, that annual savings will add up. Getting to the bottom line, assuming Roy and Tami live until 90 (a retirement of 25 years), savings will mount from using Strategy B by age 80 and age 90 as shown in the following chart:

### Roy and Tami 1.0 Taxes Owed (Cumulative)

| Strategy A | Strategy B |
|---|---|
| Total taxes owed by age 80: $6,200 | $0 |
| Total taxes owed by age 90: $16,533 | $0 |

The savings using Strategy B are striking:

**Savings Using Strategy B By:**
    **Age 80:  $6,200 (100 percent)**
    **Age 90:  $16,533 (100 percent)**

The savings to age 80 are over $6,000. In fact, Roy and Tami will owe *no taxes at all* on their withdrawals through age 80 using Strategy B. That's extra money that can pay for unexpected expenses in retirement, or charity, or a nice cruise for two, including airfare.

The savings are more than double that by age 90: $16,533. Roy and Tami never owe taxes in retirement under Strategy B. Taxes under Strategy A are not huge, but they add up. Roy and Tami eliminate 100 percent of the $16,533 tax burden of Strategy A that accumulates by age 90. Again, that is money now available for any purpose Roy and Tami want. Another cruise, anyone?

Moreover, this extra cash is all available without any additional risk. All without buying new investments that involve commissions or other fees. All without changing *anything* about the accounts except how much is taken out each year for spending.

Oh, and there is a bonus too: Roy and Tami have more money left in Buckets 1 and 2 at age 90 using Strategy B than they will if they use Strategy A (Bucket 2 increases from $0 to $30,592). Strategy B has $260,000 left at age 90, about $16,000 more than what remains using Strategy A. That makes sense because saving on taxes should mean they have more money left.

The calculations in this example and all the other examples used in this book (there are many) come from a Retirement Tax Saver system used to simulate tax treatment of retirement withdrawals up to age 90. The numbers are (of course) *estimates* of taxes owed. Actual taxes owed will vary depending, for example, on exactly how the IRS winds up adjusting tax brackets for inflation over the coming years. Using the approximations, which are based on hundreds of calculations run by the Retirement Tax Saver system for each scenario, we can do a fair job of *comparing* various withdrawal strategies.

While the exact amount of the tax savings will vary, the comparisons give approximate tax savings as measured by today's dollars (in other words, without getting distorted by estimates of future inflation rates). Even more importantly, the comparisons enabled by the Retirement Tax Saver can help identify whether one withdrawal approach is likely to save taxes when compared to another. Here, for example, it showed that starting withdrawals from Bucket 1 before age 75 is likely to save taxes versus waiting to use Bucket 1 until RMDs are required. That's very important and helpful information, even if the exact amount of the tax savings is only approximated.

If you are like Roy and Tami, you could stop reading the book right now, adopt a strategy that involves withdrawing the standard deduction from the first year of retirement, and declare victory.

Roy and Tami hit the jackpot by using their standard deduction as their pre-RMD age withdrawal from Bucket 1. But let's try a few different pre-age 75 withdrawal amounts from Bucket 1 using Strategy B and see what happens.

## Other "Roy And Tami 1.0" Scenarios
## Cumulative Taxes owed by Ages 80 and 90

### Strategy A

| Taxes owed by age 80 | Taxes owed by age 90 |
|---|---|
| $6,200 | $16,533 |

## Strategy B
## (at different Bucket 1 withdrawal rates ages 65-71)

|  | Taxes owed by age 80 | Taxes owed by age 90 |
|---|---|---|
| $20,000/year | $0 | $476 |
| **$30,700/year** | **$0** | **$0** |
| $40,000/year | $9,300 | $9,300 |

Of course Roy and Tami couldn't do better at different withdrawal rates—they already owed nothing as it is. But other pre-RMD withdrawals also saved big on taxes, just not as much. Without running the test for every possible withdrawal amount, the results seem to confirm that using the standard deduction as the withdrawal target is an effective way for Roy and Tami to go.

### *What if Roy and Tami have Social Security and Other Income? Meet Roy and Tami Version 2.0*

The prior analysis showed how using the Bucket 1 (401(k)) account before RMDs are required can reduce taxes for a couple like Roy and Tami who have only two sources of retirement income: Bucket 1 (401(k) and IRA) and Bucket 2 (already-taxed savings not in a 401(k) or IRA). Roy and Tami seem nice, but they have a pretty simple financial situation. Many if not most people in the Smart Savers category will have other sources of income in retirement, most notably Social Security. They may also have dividend and interest income from their already-taxed account which will be taxed in the year it is received.

Let's change Roy and Tami's financial picture to include these additional income sources and call them Roy and Tami version 2.0. In this version, Tami will start collecting $36,000 in Social Security at age 70, and the couple will make $5,000 in interest and dividend income every year in retirement. In view of these additional income sources, Roy and Tami increase their target annual income from $40,000 to $75,000 as shown below:

## Roy and Tami
## (Version 2.0—add Social Security and other income)

| | |
|---|---|
| **Bucket 1 (401(k)/IRA)** account balance at retirement: | $900,000 |
| **Bucket 2 (already taxed)** account balance at retirement: | $400,000 |
| **Retirement Ages:** | 65 |
| **Social Security (combined):** | $36,000/ year at age 70 |
| **Dividends/interest:** | $5,000/year |
| **Target income:** | $75,000/year |

The higher income levels will lead to higher taxes. Can we also get higher savings using different withdrawal approaches in retirement? Before we answer that, let's take a quick look at how Social Security is taxed.

### Taxing Social Security

*To determine what part of your Social Security income is treated as taxable income, the IRS looks at something it invented called "provisional income." Provisional income generally includes all other taxable income, plus one-half of your Social Security. It is just a tool used to decide what percentage of your Social Security will be taxed.*

*Social Security is not taxed if provisional income is below $32,000. If provision income is above $32,000 but below $44,000 for married couples, then 50 percent of the smaller of two numbers is added to taxable income: (1) Social Security benefits and (2) provisional income minus $32,000. For provisional income above $44,000, the smaller of two numbers is treated as taxable income: (1) 85 percent of Social Security or (2) $6,000 plus 85 percent of (provisional income minus $44,000).*[28]

*These percentages can easily get confused with tax rates, which are also expressed in percentages. But they are quite different. The 85 percent and 50 percent figures are* **not** *tax rates. For example, if you have $10,000 in Social Security, and your provisional income is $38,000, then at most half of the $10,000 or $5,000 of the Social Security income is subject to tax. The tax rate* **applied to** *that portion of Social Security income, however, could vary from 0% to 37% depending on your total taxable income.*

*This formula can result in odd effects from slight changes in additional income if your provisional income falls between $32,000 and $44,000. See "Road to higher taxes? Also paved with good intentions," by Janet Kidd Stewart, from Orlando Sentinel, April 8, 2013, https://www.pressreader.com/usa/orlando-sentin el/20130408/282252367997483.*

*The Retirement Tax Saver automatically runs an approximation of these Social Security calculations (approximate because it does not adjust for things like tax-exempt interest). The calculator also provides an adjustment because, unlike tax brackets, the provisional income formula has never been adjusted for inflation.*

---

28   Social Security Administration, "Program Provisions and SSA Administrative Data," 2019, Table 2.A31, https://www.ssa.gov/policy/docs/statcomps/supplement/2019/2a29-2a32.html.

## Roy and Tami version 2.0

### Strategy A: Conventional Wisdom Approach

Bucket 1 assets at 74: $769,249
Bucket 2 assets at 74: $0
RMD at 75: $31,270

**Cumulative taxes owed to age 74: $10,751**
**Taxes owed at 74: $3,217**

Even though Roy and Tami use Strategy A in this example, they cannot wait until age 75 to draw from Bucket 1. That is because Bucket 2 is exhausted at age 70, so Bucket 1 withdrawals begin at age 70 even though RMDs are not required until 75. Roy and Tami pay over $10,000 in taxes by age 74. Each year after age 74, withdrawals from Bucket 1 will exceed the RMDs, moreover, to pay taxes and/or to meet the income target.

If we run the Retirement Tax Saver calculator for future years, we find the total tax burden adds up as follows:

### Strategy A: Conventional Wisdom Approach

| | |
|---|---|
| **Taxes owed through age 80:** | **$34,114** |
| **Taxes owed through age 90:** | **$77,922** |

The taxes owed are quite a jump from Roy and Tami version 1.0—the additional taxable income from Social Security and other sources really adds up over time. We can see the effect of moving from the 0% tax bucket to higher tax rate buckets: cumulative taxes by age 90 leap from $16,533 to $77,922. The difference, almost quadruple, equals more than $3,000 per year from age 65 to 90.

But we digress. The critical issue is, can Strategy B also reduce taxes for Roy and Tami 2.0? With Strategy B, we start by testing a scenario that targets the maximum taxable income in the pre-age 75 years before tax liability arises. For Roy and Tami, this means they should withdraw the amount of the standard deduction for a couple aged 65, $30,700, minus $5,000/year they receive in other taxable income, for a net total of $25,700 from Bucket 1 each year before age 75. In the pre-70 years, they make up the remaining income needed, $44,300, from Bucket 2 to get to $70,000 in income. Social Security begins at age 70 at $36,000/year. At that point the Bucket 2 withdrawals drop by $36,000 to $3,300 (plus taxes owed). For ages 70 to 75, this approach will generate more taxable income than the standard deduction, and thus create some taxable income.

Here is the snapshot at 75:

### Roy and Tami 2.0

### Strategy B:(Withdraw $25,700/year
from Bucket 1 before age 75)

Bucket 1 assets at 74: $643,000
Bucket 2 assets at 74: $131,488
RMD at 75: $26,138

| | |
|---|---|
| **Taxes owed to age 80:** | **$17,227** |
| Savings vs. Strategy A: | $16,887 |
| **Taxes owed to age 90:** | **$44,650** |
| Savings vs. Strategy A: | $33,373 |

*Taxes are lower using Strategy B than under the Conventional Wisdom approach.* Roy and Tami save more than 40 percent of their growing tax liability by using Strategy B instead of Strategy A. While the *percentages* aren't as impressive as with Roy and Tami version 1.0, the *dollars* are significantly more.

Let's try a few other target Bucket 1 withdrawal amounts, and see what the cumulative tax savings are at ages 80 and 90:

## Roy and Tami 2.0

### Other Strategy B withdrawal rates

|  | Taxes owed by 80 | Taxes owed by 90 |
|---|---|---|
| **Strategy A** ($0) | $34,114 | $77,922 |
| **Strategy B (Annual Bucket 1 withdrawal)** | | |
| $15,000 | $21,938 | $56,190 |
| **$25,700** | **$17,227** | $44,650 |
| **$35,000** | $27,267 | **$41,169** |
| $45,000 | $38,758 | $42,673 |
| $55,000 | $49,120 | $49,120 |

The $25,700 target we already used is best among the tested options for saving taxes by age 80. A $35,000 withdrawal rate, however, saves about $5,000 more in taxes by age 90 ($36,753 savings vs. Strategy A). That is once again money that is available without risk and by merely adjusting withdrawals made from each of Bucket 1 and Bucket 2.

### *Roy and Tami Version 3.0:*
### *Grow accounts 3 percent per year after inflation*

So far, our Roy-and-Tami examples have assumed that their Bucket 1 and Bucket 2 accounts do not appreciate or depreciate compared to inflation. You might say, that's all well and good, but I have invested my accounts and expect them to grow faster than inflation over time. To address that scenario, let's model Roy and Tami version 3.0, which is like Roy and Tami 2.0 except we assume those accounts grow 3 percent per year. We would expect to see higher taxes, but will we see a change in savings as well?

Let's compare Strategy A to Strategy B using a variety of withdrawal rates:

### Roy and Tami 3.0

|  | Taxes owed by 80 | Taxes owed by 90 |
|---|---|---|
| **Strategy A** | $42,870 | $112,040 |
| **Strategy B (Annual Bucket 1 withdrawal before age 75)** | | |
| $15,000 | $32,859 | $97,321 |
| 25,000 | $34,312 | $91,360 |
| **$25,700** | **$34,312** | $91,067 |
| $35,000 | $42,285 | $91,935 |
| $55,000 | $57,566 | $83,921 |
| $75,000 | $73,120 | $76,580 |
| **$85,000** | $85,345 | **$85,345** |

Initial observations: Because we added appreciation, a number of values go up. The accounts have a lot more left by age 90. Strategy A taxes go up when we assume a modest 3 percent growth rate over inflation. Thank compounding and RMDs for that.

Now for the question at hand: Can Strategy B help us reduce the growing taxes due to appreciating accounts? In short, yes. For taxes through age 80, Strategy B provides benefits of about $8,000 or about 20 percent in saved taxes when using $25,700 as the target Bucket 1 withdrawal amount annual before RMD age. For cumulative taxes owed by age 90, savings compared to Strategy A grow to about $21,000 or 19 percent. Roy and Tami save enough for a cruise, airfare, and more (depending on the cruise). It may not be enough to change lifestyles, and as a percentage of taxes owed it is not as impressive a reduction as with the prior scenarios. But the fact that the extra $8,000 or $21,000 comes with no extra risk, no new investments, and no fees still makes it a compelling why-not decision for retirement withdrawals.

When we try other withdrawal amounts, it turns out that a $75,000 withdrawal rate before age 75 provides even better tax performance by age 90: The total taxes owed of about $76,000 *is about $36,000 less than with the wait-til-72+ strategy—a savings of about 32 percent!* This might be a little startling and confusing because our targeted level of income is only $75,000, yet the best strategy for the long term is to withdraw *more than is needed* for income in the years leading up to age 75. With Strategy B at a $75,000 withdrawal rate, in the pre-75 years the 401(k) withdrawal is so large that some part of the distribution is not needed to pay income or taxes. Between ages 65 and 69 the excess totals $25,000 each year. Then, after Social Security kicks in, the excess surges to $61,000 at ages 70 and 71.

What is going on? This scenario involves paying higher taxes in the early years in order to dramatically reduce taxes in later years. Social Security is not taxed as heavily in the post-age 75 years as well, increasing the tax benefits of early withdrawals from Bucket 1. Ideally, Roy and Tami put each year's excess amount into a Roth IRA. Roth IRAs have many benefits: the account grows tax-free forever into the future, *and* the money is tax-free when it is withdrawn. It also is not subject to a RMD payment. It has some estate planning advantages too.[29] The

---

29 Fidelity, "Compelling reasons to consider a Roth IRA," Apr. 28, 2021, https://www.fidelity.com/learning-center/personal-finance/retirement/nine-reasons-roth.

opportunity to create tax-efficient Roth conversions like this is yet another potential bonus from implementing Strategy B at withdrawal rates that exceed income needs.

There is always a catch—here, it is the fact that the conversion from a regular IRA or 401(k) to a Roth account is treated as taxable income in the year the conversion happens. But our Retirement Tax Saver calculations show that we come out way ahead if we withdraw this excess even though it is taxable, because it will reduce RMDS in the years after 75 significantly. The pros outweigh the cons for Roy and Tami version 3.0 to do Roth conversions between ages 65 and 75.

It may feel strange to voluntarily increase your taxable income in the pre-RMD years. After a working lifetime of paying income taxes, you might relish the thought of keeping your taxable income in early retirement so low that you pay no income taxes, regardless of its impact on taxes owed in future years. I can't deny that would be a great feeling. And if your primary goal is to pay the smallest possible taxes *that year*, then the strategies of this book may not work for you. I would only suggest, however, that such an approach is too focused on winning short-term battles and not focused enough on winning the long-term war. The numbers speak for themselves on that front.

### Other Variations

Roy and Tami save, you might note, but your situation is different from Roy's and Tami's. What about other couples in other financial situations? Are Roy and Tami a special case? There are an infinite number of variations, and we can't address them all here. If this same approach lowers taxes in enough different situations, however, the odds go up that it will save taxes in *your* situation. In the next chapter we will meet another couple, Pat and Chris, to answer this question at least in part.

While the above analysis provides some clear options for Roy and Tami, your situation is different. If the numbers change, are taxes still lower under Strategy B? The short answer to this important question is, "probably, but it depends." The number of variations on an individual's or couple's financial situation in retirement is infinite. The Retirement Tax Saver tool will, however, help customize the answer for a situation more closely tailored to your unique situation.

If you appreciate the principle behind Strategy B, however, you may have a good idea of whether it would reduce taxes in your specific situation. The principle is the "use it or lose it" discussed earlier in the book. In the vast majority of situations, it will make sense to "use" and "not lose" the chance to get, for example, $27,700 in taxable income ($30,700 if you are married and over 65) for $0 in taxes by withdrawing that amount from Bucket 1 in the retirement years after age 59½ (the earliest for unconditionally penalty-free withdrawals from 401(k)s and IRAs) and before RMD age.

# Chapter Five

## More Examples of Ways to Save—Account Values $1.5 million-$3 million, with Savings up to $170,000

To recap, last chapter we showed examples of how *accelerating* withdrawals from Bucket 1—your 401(k) money that Conventional Wisdom says to *delay* using as long as possible— can save tens of thousands of dollars in taxes. We illustrated this by focusing on a couple whose retirement assets total $1.3 million. We showed how our fictional couple, Roy and Tami, could save thousands of dollars in taxes by doing nothing more than withdrawing more money from Bucket 1 and less money from Bucket 2 in the years before RMDs begin.

To select how much to withdraw from Bucket 1 before age 75, we used the standard deduction for couples over 65 ($30,700) as our guide. Using this amount, Roy and Tami version 1.0 (with no additional sources of income) went from paying $6,200 in taxes to paying $0—nada, zilch—by age 80. They went from $16,533 to $0, saving 100 percent of their total tax bill owed, by age 90. All without any change in their investments or accounts.

When we added other sources of income such as Social Security (Roy and Tami version 2.0), the savings were reduced as a percentage. However, Roy and Tami could still save thousands by age 80 and over $36,000 by age 90. When we added 3% appreciation of their accounts over inflation, the tax savings held steady at $36,000 by age 90. That's savings that simply cannot be ignored. And they saved merely by changing when they withdraw from the accounts they already have.

Pretty easy, wouldn't you say?

You might, but you might also wonder whether this approach can save taxes for financial situations (like yours, probably) that are much different than Roy and Tami's. What happens, for example, if their Bucket 1 and Bucket 2 accounts are bigger? Will savings go up, go down, stay the same, or disappear?

Let's find out.

### *Meet Pat and Chris*

Pat and Chris have $2 million in a collection of IRAs and 401(k)s (Bucket 1) and $1 million in a collection of regular accounts (Bucket 2). They are each 65 years old. Pat and Chris's assets in Bucket 1 and Bucket 2 are more than double Roy and Tami's (version 1.0), leading us to increase their target after-tax income to $100,000 per year. To simplify the comparison between Conventional Wisdom Strategy A and Strategy B, at least initially assume they have no Social Security or other income and no appreciation after taxes in their accounts.

### Pat and Chris 1.0

**Bucket 1 balance at retirement: $2 million**
**Bucket 2 balance at retirement: $1 million**
**Retirement Ages: 65**
**Target annual income: $100,000**

If Pat and Chris use Conventional Wisdom (Strategy A) and wait to use Bucket 1 as long as possible, then they would withdraw $100,000 from Bucket 2 each year from 65 to 75, their

RMD ages. That's $1,000,000 over ten years, leaving nothing. No taxes owed. So far so good.

But at 75, that changes. The RMDs on Bucket 1 (which is untouched) will be $2 million divided by 24.6, or $81,301. Pat and Chris will need an additional $17,007, however, from Bucket 2 to get to $100,000 in income. Federal income taxes will be $8,950. For this and all other scenarios used in this book, taxes are paid from the already-taxed account Bucket 2 unless it reaches a $0 balance, at which point the 401(k) account is used (which itself would result in additional taxes being owed).

Here's the snapshot of this Conventional Wisdom scenario:

### Pat and Chris 1.0

### Strategy A: Conventional Wisdom Approach

Bucket 1 assets at 75: $2 million
Bucket 2 assets at 75: $300,000
RMD at 75: $81,301

**Taxes owed 65-74: $0**
**Taxes owed at 75: $8,950**

If we run the tax calculator for future years, we find the total tax burden adds up as follows:

**Taxes owed through age 80: $53,700**
**Taxes owed through age 90: $143,200**

Now, let's have Pat and Chris try a Strategy B approach that involves withdrawing from Bucket 1 starting at 65 instead of waiting until 75. They withdraw the amount of the standard deduction for a couple aged 65, $30,700, from the IRA each year before age 75, and make up the remaining income needed, $69,300, from Bucket 2.

Here is the snapshot at 75:

## Pat and Chris 1.0

### Strategy B ($30,700/year in Bucket 1 withdrawals up to age 75)

Bucket 1 assets at 75: $1,693,000
Bucket 2 assets at 75: $307,000
RMD at 75: $68,821

**Taxes owed 65-74: $0**
**Taxes owed at 75: $4,135**
**Taxes saved at 75 (one year): $4,815**
**Taxes owed to age 80: $24,118**
**Taxes owed to age 90: $100,820**

Savings arise right away at age 75 to the tune of $4,815. The Bucket 1 withdrawal drops from $100,000 to $68,821—over $30,000 less. Because the already-taxed account has plenty of money in it, we use that account to make up the difference. That difference in RMDs is taxed at 12%. Pat and Chris **save $4,815 in annual taxes at age 75.** That's after paying no taxes between 65 and 75, just like the Conventional Wisdom strategy of deferring Bucket 1 withdrawals until RMDs are due. The entire $4,815 per year appears to be *pure savings*.

Wait, there's more good news. What happens to taxes owed after 75 when we use Strategy B at $30,700/year? They are *lower* than under the Conventional Wisdom approach—as we saw for Roy and Tami version 1.0. Bucket 1 assets dropped in value about $300,000, lowering the RMD. When we add the taxes paid over several years, we get the following:

74

## Pat and Chris 1.0 Savings using Strategy B ($30,700) vs. Strategy A

**Total taxes paid by age 80: Save $29,582**
**Total taxes paid by age 90: Save $42,380**

The savings to age 80 total about $30,000 (about 56 percent). That's enough for an upgraded room for two on Roy and Tami's cruise, including airfare. The savings top $42,000 by age 90 (about 30 percent).

All without any additional risk. All without buying new investments. All without changing *anything* about the accounts except how much is taken out each year for spending.

Before we try other scenarios, let's make a few more adjustments to Pat and Chris's situation to reflect Social Security, other income, and appreciation as we did for Roy and Tami. Meet Pat and Chris 3.0 (we will skip version 2.0 just to keep things moving):

### Pat and Chris 3.0

| | |
|---|---|
| **Add Social Security (combined):** | **$36,000 starting at age 70** |
| **Add other income:** | **increase to $15,000** |
| **Target annual income:** | **increase to $170,000/year** |

**3 percent annual post-inflation appreciation rate**

In view of the higher income targeted, we will be mindful of additional tax bracket break points: not just the $30,700 (standard deduction) we used previously, but also $50,000 (about the break point from 10% to 12% tax rate) and $120,150 (break point from 12% to 22% tax rate). We will also keep in mind the $15,000 in other income that Pat and Chris receive each year.

Without further ado, here are the numbers using Strategy A and Strategy B at various tax bracket-based withdrawal rates:

## Pat and Chris 3.0

### Taxes owed using Strategies A and B

|  | Taxes owed by 80 | Taxes owed by 90 |
|---|---|---|
| **Strategy A** | $212,477 | $469,823 |
| **Strategy B** (withdrawals pre-75 from Bucket 1) | | |
| $20,000/year | $180,314 | $437,660 |
| **$50,000/year** | **$138,064** | $389,500 |
| **$120,150/year** | $217,157 | **$308,060** |

The first thing you may notice is that Chris and Pat owe a lot more taxes than Roy and Tami did. Good catch. That's our progressive tax system at work. Seeing the numbers added up over several years might produce sticker shock. The taxes owed over the years are enough to buy a nice house.

The next thing to notice, with greater happiness: the best Strategy B target withdrawal amount we selected produces *over $160,000 in tax savings* by age 90 when compared to Strategy A. The savings total about 35 percent, or about $162,000 at a $120,150 withdrawal rate. By age 80, we see savings of about $74,000 or over 35% using the $50,000 withdrawal rate, but savings are much more modest by age 90 at this withdrawal rate than they are for the $120,150 withdrawal rate. Sound the trumpets as we compare these numbers and show the savings:

## Pat and Chris 3.0

### Tax Savings Strategy B vs. Strategy A

| Strategy B | by age 80 | by age 90 |
|---|---|---|
| **$50,000/year withdrawals** | **$74,413** | $80,323 |
| $120,150/year withdrawals | ($4,860) | $161,763 |

These numbers are not the taxes *owed*. They are they taxes *saved* by using Strategy B at these withdrawal rates instead of Strategy A. Imagine what Pat and Chris could do with and extra $161,763! Moreover, the account balances left at age 90 (in today's dollars) under Strategy A are $749,893 in Bucket 1 and $0 in Bucket 2. Under Strategy B at $120,150/year withdrawals, at age 90 Bucket 1 increases to $787,869 and Bucket 2 increases to $119,696. As expected, lower taxes leave more money in the bank.

Should we get greedy? Let's play with a few more withdrawal amounts above and below these bracket-based amounts. We cover a wide range of numbers and highlight the lowest-tax numbers for age 80 and age 90.

### Pat and Chris 3.0 other Strategy B withdrawal rates

| Target withdrawal | Taxes owed by 80 | Taxes owed by 90 |
|---|---|---|
| **Strategy A** | $212,477 | $469,823 |

| Target withdrawal | Taxes owed by 80 | Taxes owed by 90 |
| --- | --- | --- |
| Strategy B | | |
| $40,000 | $156,597 | $413,994 |
| $80,000 | $157,182 | $318,903 |

The savings using the alternative numbers are not as good as they were for the numbers based on tax brackets. This suggests that, while trial and error can help us find the best numbers by brute force, if we want to quickly zero in on the better withdrawal rates, the tax bracket break points hold up well as good annual withdrawal rates to look at initially for some of the best tax savings.

If your retirement assets are in the ballpark of Chris and Pat's, you just found out how to make your retirement assets last longer and work harder for you in retirement. All by just doing exactly what the tax rules encourage you to do—start taking withdrawals from your 401(k) and IRA accounts before you reach RMD age. The government will be happy to see you generate taxable income this way sooner than you would have otherwise. You are just following the IRS's lead. There's nothing untoward about that. Reap the benefits of Strategy B with a clear conscience!

### Bonus Idea: Strategy B Also Helps Deal with "Straggler" Tax-deferred Accounts

Do you have multiple tax-deferred accounts? New accounts can pop up for a variety of reasons. Switching jobs can result in new accounts. Or a bank or other financial institution you do business with may have had a tax-deferred account option that caught your eye, so you decided to put some money into it. Over the course of twenty or thirty years, many of us accumulated multiple accounts, some of which have much smaller balances than others. Those little lingering accounts are the stragglers.

There are ways to consolidate accounts to eliminate stragglers, such as a rollover. But human beings what we are, we sometimes procrastinate on doing things (like consolidating) that we know we "should" do. The end result is that, sometimes, those smaller straggler accounts can linger for years.

I'm not here to judge. Let he or she who is without sin cast the first stone. But I am here to suggest a solution to this little annoyance: You can implement Strategy B by using your straggler tax-deferred accounts first. That will give you even more satisfaction from implementing these strategies as it will also wind up streamlining your balance sheet!

### What if Pat and Chris Take Social Security Sooner?

You may have noticed that in the version 2.0 and 3.0 scenarios used so far, we assumed our couples would defer starting Social Security until age 70. Regular retirement age is 67, when you can take your base monthly benefit. However, the Social Security Administration (SSA) gives you options: you can start as early as 62, or as late as 70. For each year you wait past 67, if you were born after 1942, your annual benefit increases by 8 percent.[30]

There's nothing tricky here. The SSA figures out the average life expectancy, and overall the SSA winds up paying out the same amount of money over everyone's lifetime regardless of the starting age. Of course, statistically speaking, very few of us individually will be "average"—we are likely to kick the bucket sooner or later than the average. If you think you will live longer or shorter than average, you might want to adjust your starting year accordingly.

---

30 Social Security Administration, "Retirement Benefits: Delayed Retirement Credits," https://www.ssa.gov/benefits/retirement/planner/delayret.html.

Given that individual situations may cause people to want to start Social Security at different times, what is the impact of changing the Social Security start date on the benefits of Strategy B? To answer that question, let's go to version 4.0 of Chris and Pat, which is just like version 3.0 except they start Social Security at age 67. If we apply the 8 percent rule, this works out to getting $28,578 at age 67 ($28,578 multiplied by (1.08) three times for each year between 67 and 70 = $36,000).

## Pat and Chris 4.0

## Start Social Security at 67 instead of 70

**Social Security starts: Age 67**
**Annual Benefit: $28,578**

|  | Taxes owed by 80 | Taxes owed by 90 |
|---|---|---|
| **Strategy A** | $197,809 | $458,294 |
| **Strategy B** |  |  |
| $40,000/year | $160,768 | $421,253 |
| $50,000/year | $134,696 | $383,063 |
| $80,000/year | $153,837 | $311,257 |
| $120,150/year | $221,706 | $305,038 |
| $140,000/year | $258,087 | $327,121 |

Interestingly, Pat and Chris's taxes to ages 80 and 90 using Strategy A go down by about $12,000 when they start Social Security sooner. It turns out that Pat and Chris can save some taxes by age 80 and age 90 if they start Social Security at 67 instead of 70 using the Conventional Wisdom approach.

However, using strategy B, the taxes go up slightly when they start Social Security at 67. For example, at a $120,150 withdrawal rate, taxes to age 90 are $308,060 if they take Social Security at 70, and $305,038 if they begin Social Security at 67. That is a difference of about $3,000, or one percent. This would suggest that we shouldn't guess what will happen to taxes if we change the Social Security start date—we need to run the numbers.

Importantly, it also turns out that Pat and Chris 4.0 can save a lot on taxes using Strategy B at the same withdrawal amounts we used for Pat and Chris 3.0, who started Social Security at age 70, almost as much as they do when they start Social Security at 70. They save about $153,000 by age 90 using the $120,150 withdrawal rate—over thirty percent of the large $460,000 tax bill they are facing with Strategy A! Does that mean Pat and Chris should not wait until 70 to begin taking Social Security? Not necessarily, but this is important additional information that will help them develop good options and make the decision. Deferring Social Security provides "old age insurance" by increasing benefits for as long as you live. Strategy B may provide "bridge" income needed to allow deferral.

The Tax Saver calculator will allow you to test differing Social Security starting years, so you can determine whether it makes a difference—and get an idea of how much of a difference—in your personal situation.

Now let's move on to another example.


### Meet Mark and Lois: Retiring Earlier, Taking Social Security Sooner

Let's meet Mark and Lois. We will pick an earlier retirement date for them: age 62. Let's change to an earlier Social Security start date as well, 67. Let's also assume both of them collect Social Security of $22,000 at age 62. We assume a 3 percent account growth rate after inflation as we did for version 3.0 of the prior couples. At 62 their finances look like the following:

### Mark and Lois

**Bucket 1 balance at retirement: $1 million**
**Bucket 2 balance at retirement: $600,000**
**Social Security: $22,000/year at age 62 (each)**
**Other income: $15,000/year**
**Retirement ages: 62**
**Target annual income: $130,000/year**
**3 percent annual post-inflation appreciation rate**

If we run the Conventional Wisdom scenario of waiting until age 75 to use the 401(k) account, as well as some Strategy B withdrawal rates, we get the following for Taxes owed by ages 80 and 90:

### "Mark and Lois" Scenarios

|  | Taxes owed by 80 | Taxes owed by 90 |
|---|---|---|
| **Strategy A** | $132,930 | $274,071 |
| **Strategy B** | | |
| $25,000/year | $114,545 | $255,686 |
| $65,000/year | $147,077 | $205,810 |
| $80,000/year | $175,217 | $188,211 |

Mark and Lois can also benefit significantly from using Strategy B instead of Strategy A, despite retiring earlier and taking Social Security earlier than our other couples. Of the Strategy B target withdrawals tested, the $80,000 Strategy

B withdrawal rate provides the greatest benefits by age 90, saving over $85,000 or over 30 percent on cumulative taxes. This benefit comes at an early price, however: by age 80, this version of Strategy B incurs about $55,000 or 40 percent *more* in taxes versus Strategy A. Still, by 90, Mark and Lois more than make up for this earlier cost, and wind up saving more than $85,000.

The turnaround by age 90 using the $80,000 Strategy B withdrawal rate arises because it draws Bucket 1 down so much in the early years. This gives rise to higher taxes on Social Security in the pre-75 years, but after 75 the RMDs stay around $10,000/year for many years. This keeps taxable income so low after age 75 that much less of Mark and Lois's Social Security is taxed in the years after age 75. This helps Mark and Lois by reducing taxable income **and** potentially reducing their *tax bracket* throughout the post-75 years.

This strategy involves moving $9,000 each year between ages 62 and 74 from Bucket 1 into Bucket 2. As discussed previously in a comparable situation, ideally this transfer would be in the form of a Roth conversion that provides substantial future benefits. The tax savings, however, do not require the use of a Roth conversion. That is just frosting on the cake.

Strategy B keeps more money in Mark and Lois' pockets. Over $85,000 more by age 90.

Just by using their existing accounts. With no additional risk. Just by implementing a simple Bucket 1 withdrawal strategy. That's hard to beat for a simple and low risk way to save money during retirement. These savings are nothing to sneeze at, especially given that Mark and Lois are working with smaller 401(k) and already-taxed accounts (Buckets 1 and 2). They indicate that Strategy B can save money with earlier Social Security and retirement beginning dates and for couples who both draw Social Security. These numbers are further confirmation that the Conventional Wisdom, Strategy

A approach incurs needless additional taxes as compared to Strategy B for retired couples in a variety of financial situations.

The numbers also show that picking the right withdrawal *amount* for Strategy B is itself a decision that can result in tens of thousands of dollars in additional tax savings. Using Strategy B is great, but the maximum benefit from this approach is achieved only if various withdrawal rates are evaluated.

# Chapter Six

## Lessons Learned, and a 70 Percent Savings Surprise for Lower Account Values

H ere is a summary of what we learned so far:

- **Conventional wisdom that says wait to withdraw from tax-deferred 401(k) and IRA accounts can be costly from a tax standpoint in retirement.** This strategy encourages waiting to withdraw from 401(k) accounts until withdrawals are required to avoid penalties, usually at age 75. We called that "Strategy A." This approach may save taxes in early years, but (a) may be no better than other approaches in early years and (b) will come back to bite you in later years when bigger 401(k) withdrawals trigger bigger tax burdens, and you have no more money in after-tax accounts to help you keep taxes lower.

- **Pre-RMD age withdrawals from your 401(k) account can provide significant tax savings by ages 80 and 90.** "Strategy B" can cost the same or only a little more in taxes in the pre-RMD years while providing significant tax savings in the years after RMD age. This have-your-cake-and-eat-it-too outcome is due to "using and not losing" the benefit of lower tax bracket withdrawals in the pre-RMD years. In our examples, the savings ranged from a few thousand dollars to over $170,000. Quite a range, but all the more reason to make sure you check your individual situation to understand how much you may be able to save using Strategy B.

- **Picking how much to withdraw pre-RMD age can be the difference between small tax savings and big tax savings.** When to withdraw from your 401(k), and how much, depends on your specific situation. You need to run the calculations using the Tax Saver to find the most beneficial withdrawal amounts.

- **Targeting tax bracket break points can be a useful way to zero in on withdrawal rates that provide the biggest tax savings.** Tax bracket break points are taxable income levels at which tax rates go up—like $30,700 for the standard deduction for married couples age 65 and over (going from 0% taxes to 10%), $52,700 (from 10% to 12%), and $120,150 (from 12% to 22%). Using one or more of these numbers tended to be close to the better withdrawal rates for lowering taxes owed by age 80 or age 90.

- **By withdrawing from Bucket 1 in the pre-RMD age years, you reduce the amount of taxable RMDs that will be due after 72. You will also have more non-taxed money available in Bucket 2 in the years after age 72.** If you use more of Bucket 1 before you reach RMD age, you will need less from Bucket 2. That means you will have more money in the good bucket (Bucket 2) and less money in the bad bucket (Bucket 1) than you would have had using the wait-til-72+ approach. That's a great trade from a tax standpoint. From RMD age on, you will have more money available to use that will not be taxed as income (Bucket 2). You will have lower RMDs and thus lower required income that leads to required taxes. Your income taxes will be lower for the rest of your life! While you may already have plenty of reasons to live a long time anyway, this will add to the list.

- **The benefits from pre-RMD age 401(k) withdrawals can exist even if you have other sources of income, such as Social Security, a pension, or dividends and interest.**

Now we will move on to one more example for a pleasant surprise for those with smaller retirement savings accounts.

### Juan and Maria: Smaller Accounts, Potentially Big Savings

Let's meet Juan and Maria. They are closer to the average for people in the "top 20 percent" mentioned in Chapter 2. They have $500,000 in a 401(k) and $300,000 in an already-taxed account. The accounts grow at 3 percent per year after inflation. They have $5,000 in other income and $30,000 in Social Security that starts at 67 (one spouse claims $20,000/year at that age, and the other claims 50 percent of that amount, or $10,000). An annual benefit of $20,000 is close to the average annual Social Security benefit.[31] Their target income is $70,000.

### Juan and Maria

**Bucket 1 account balance at retirement: $500,000**
**Bucket 2 account balance at retirement: $300,000**
**Social Security: $30,000/year at age 67 (combined)**

31  AARP Retirement Social Security Resource Center, "How much Social Security will I get?" https://www.aarp.org/retirement/social-security/questions-answers/how-much-social-security-will-i-get.html. The site notes that the average Social Security retirement benefit in 2021 is $1,543 per month.

**Other income: $5,000/year**
**Retirement ages: 65**
**Target annual income: $70,000/year**
**3 percent annual post-inflation appreciation rate**

|  | Taxes owed by 80 | Taxes owed by 90 |
| --- | --- | --- |
| **Strategy A** | $29,839 | $71,770 |
| **Strategy B** | | |
| $20,000/year | $1,650 | $27,735 |
| $30,000/year | $15,749 | $20,793 |
| $40,000/year | $34,967 | $34,967 |

These tables show some significant savings versus Strategy A if they use Strategy B at $30,000: over $14,000 in tax savings by age 80 and almost $51,000, or 71 percent, by age 90. The savings are especially impressive because the overall taxes owed by Juan and Maria are lower than for our previous example couples. Had we assumed that lower account values and target income necessarily resulted in relatively lower savings, we would have been wrong. Also, shifting from Strategy A to Strategy B at $30,000/year withdrawals leaves more money in Juan and Maria's accounts. Bucket 1's remaining balance at age 90 in today's dollars increases from $112,697 to $174,829.

Here, the dramatic savings can be explained in large part by the taxation of Juan and Maria's Social Security benefits. Using Strategy A, Juan and Maria's Bucket 1 withdrawals are large enough to result in significant taxation of their Social Security in the years after age 75. Strategy B at a $30,000 withdrawal rate, however, keeps Bucket 1 withdrawals after 75 low enough to significantly reduce taxation of Social Security.

Below we see how different Bucket 1 withdrawals affect "provisional income" used to calculate the percentage of Social Security income that will be taxed:

### Juan and Maria's provisional income at 74
### (After Bucket 2 runs out using Strategy A at age 73)

| Source | Provisional Income |
|---|---|
| Social Security: | $15,000 (50 percent) + |
| Other income: | $5,000 + |
| Bucket 2: | $0 + |
| Bucket 1: | $35,000 + |
| **Total Provisional Income:** | **$55,000** |

Because Juan and Maria's provisional income *exceeds* *$42,000*, they are taxed on the lesser of 85 percent of their Social Security benefits or $6,000 plus 85 percent of the provisional income exceeding $42,000. That totals $15,350 in 2021 dollars in our example:

### Taxable portion of Juan and Maria
### Social Security with Strategy A:

Lesser of:
1. 85 percent of $30,000 Social Security benefit = ($25,500), or
2. $6,000 + 85 percent of ($55,000 - $44,000) = **($15,350)**

The Retirement Tax Saver calculator adjusts these numbers for future years—this calculation is just a simplified illustration.

In contrast, Juan and Maria using Strategy B at a $30,000 withdrawal rate have less in Bucket 1 and more in Bucket 2 beyond age 73, lowering provisional income after 73. The difference is big enough that a much smaller percentage of Social Security is taxed. At age 74, for example, their income using Strategy B looks like the following:

### Juan and Maria's provisional income at age 75 (Using Strategy B at a $30,000/year withdrawal rate until 75)

| Source | Provisional Income |
|---|---|
| Social Security: | (50 percent) $15,000 + |
| Other income: | $5,000 + |
| Bucket 2: | $0 + |
| Bucket 1: | $12,916 |
| **Total Provisional Income:** | **$32,916** |

With Strategy B at $30,000/year Juan and Maria's provisional income is much lower (again using simplified calculations). Their provisional income is just $916 over the $32,000 threshold, meaning that only 50% times $916 or $458 of Social Security is taxed instead of $15,350. This results in a much smaller portion of their Social Security being taxed. That is a dramatic difference for them.

In the years after age 75, the Bucket 1 withdrawal will change but, in most years it keeps provisional income low. Because provisional income brackets do not adjust for inflation, their provisional income should continue to rise each year, but even then, no more than 50 percent of Social Security is taxed, not 85 percent, so long as provisional income stays below $44,000.

This $14,942 reduction in taxable Social Security income in this example year represents a significant reduction. This reduction has significant consequences for the taxation of Juan and Maria's Social Security, and their overall taxes over the course of their retirement.

For our prior couples, their provisional income usually was high enough that it was common that 85 percent was used for taxation calculations regardless of the strategy used. But Juan and Maria can manage Social Security taxation, providing the opportunity for larger tax savings—or the trap of needless extra taxation if withdrawals are *not* well managed.

At first glance, we might have assumed that, because Juan and Maria have smaller retirement accounts than Roy and Tami or Pat and Chris, they would benefit less from a withdrawal strategy. However, when Social Security considerations are thrown in, it turns out that the Strategy B withdrawal strategies may provide even **more** help for couples like Juan and Maria, who have near a million dollars in their retirement accounts and are looking forward to receiving Social Security benefits. Who knew?

OK, this couple's party has now grown to four couples. It's been nice to meet Roy, Tami, Chris, Pat, Mark, Lois, Juan, and Maria. We will take a quick look at couples with two Social Security checks each month in the next chapter and single filers in the following chapter. After that, we will send all of these nice people home and figure out which approach works best for *you*.

# Chapter Seven

## Married with Savings—Saving with a Second Social Security Benefit and Different Ages

What if spouses start collecting Social Security at different ages? The strategies for how and when to claim Social Security in that scenario can get complicated. Whatever you decide to do, the good news is that the strategies outlined in this book still work, and the Retirement Tax Saver will help guide you to a good option.

For spouses who start claiming Social Security benefits in the same calendar year, they may simply add their benefits together to represent the Social Security annual distribution as used in the Retirement Tax Saver. What happens, however, if the spouses claim different start dates? The Retirement Tax Saver gives you the option of inputting two different Social Security starting ages and benefit amounts.

This scenario also benefits from consideration of Strategy B. We can see this from an example. Let's start with revisiting our friends Juan and Maria, with some changes. Maria is three years younger than Juan and will pull down $20,000 in annual Social Security benefits as compared to Juan's $30,000. Both will begin collecting at age 67. Let's call this version 5.0:

## Juan and Maria 5.0

Bucket 1 account balance at retirement: $500,000
Bucket 2 account balance at retirement: $300,000
Retirement Ages: 65 (Juan), 62 (Maria)
Social Security: Juan: $30,000 starting at age 67
Maria: $20,000 starting at age 67
Other income: $5,000
Target annual income: $85,000/year
3 percent annual post-inflation appreciation rate

Here's how Juan and Maria 5.0's tax bill looks with each strategy:

|  | Taxes owed by 80 | Taxes owed by 90 |
|---|---|---|
| **Strategy A:** | $37,361 | $79,193 |
| **Strategy B** | | |
| $20,000/year: | $10,784 | $50,586 |
| **$30,000/year** | **$21,291** | $38,536 |
| $40,000/year | $40,067 | $40,127 |

Juan and Maria will save using Strategy B: about $16,000 in taxes by age 80 and $40,000 in taxes by age 90 using a $30,000 withdrawal rate. The age 90 savings equal 49 percent of the total tax bill of Strategy A. They can save by age 80 (73%) using a $20,000 withdrawal rate, but at higher taxes by age 90 compared to taxes at a $30,000/year withdrawal rate. Either amount for an annual target Bucket 1 withdrawal is a significant improvement over Strategy A's Conventional Wisdom. This is an example of how tax savings arise even when the parameters regarding age and Social Security change.

A married couple with two monthly Social Security checks may find it especially tempting to postpone use of the tax-deferred (Bucket 1) accounts until distributions are required. Whether a married couple collects one or two Social Security checks each month, however, they may lower their taxes by using Strategy B for withdrawals in retirement instead of waiting to draw from tax-deferred 401(k) and IRA accounts until they reach RMD age.

Now that we have run a wide variety of scenarios that show tax savings for married couples, let's take a quick look at single filers to confirm they can save with strategic withdrawals too.

# Chapter Eight

## Single Scoop—Single Savvy Savers May Also Save $100,000 or More Using a Smart Withdrawal Strategy

In prior chapters we demonstrated how using Strategy B can save taxes versus Conventional Wisdom with various scenarios involving married couples filing jointly. It should come as no surprise that those filing as singles (or in other categories for that matter) will also be able to lower their taxes using Strategy B. While the numbers change for singles tax brackets versus married filing jointly, the tax rates are the same, and the overall structure of the tax brackets is the same.

Here are the tax brackets and rates for single filers:

### Single Individual Tax Brackets 2023

| Income | Rate |
| --- | --- |
| $0 - $13,850 (age 65, $15,700) | 0% |
| Next $11,000 (up to $26,700 if age 65) | 10% |
| Next $33,725 (to $60,425) | 12% |
| Next $50,650 (to $111,075) | 22% |
| Next $86,725 (to $197,800) | 24% |

| Next $49,150 (to $246,950) | 32% |
| Next $346,875 (to $593,825) | 35% |
| Above $593,825 | 37% |

The bracket cutoffs equal half the cutoffs of the brackets for married filing jointly, except at the 35% and 37% levels. The IRS adjusts these numbers for inflation annually, just like they do for married couples filing jointly.

The brackets for calculating taxable portions of Social Security also change. Instead of using $32,000 and $44,000 as the cutoffs, single filers use $25,000 and $34,000. Similar to married couples filing jointly, the IRS does not adjust these numbers for inflation for single filers.

Let's try some examples using single filing status. These examples will give a sense of the scope of the savings possible for singles, and provide some guidance as to the numbers to try when evaluating Strategy B. We will start, as we did with the married filing jointly examples, with a simple scenario which involves no Social Security or other income and no assumed appreciation of the accounts.

### *Singles Example 1: Meet Aaron—Retirement Accounts Totaling $700,000*

Aaron has $400,000 in an IRA (Bucket 1) and $300,000 in a regular account (Bucket 2). He is 65 years old. He wants $25,000 in income each year. He has no Social Security or other income, and his accounts do not grow over inflation.

## Aaron 1.0 (Simple example)

**Bucket 1 account balance at retirement: $400,000**
**Bucket 2 account balance at retirement: $300,000**
**Retirement age: 65**
**Target annual income: $25,000/year**

Let's try Strategy A: wait until RMDs begin at age 75 before withdrawing from traditional IRA and 401(k) tax-deferred accounts (Conventional Wisdom). Here's the snapshot of the Strategy A scenario:

### Aaron 1.0

### Strategy A: Conventional Wisdom
### (Wait to withdraw from Bucket 1)

Bucket 1 assets at age 74 (end): $400,000
Bucket 2 assets at age 74 (end): $50,000
(withdraw $25,000/year from 65 to 74)
RMD (Bucket 1) at 75: $16,260
Bucket 2 withdrawal at 75: $8,740

**Taxes owed 65-74: $0**
**Taxes owed at 75: $56**
**Taxes owed (cumulative) to age 80: $642**
**Taxes owed (cumulative) to age 90: $10,999**

### Strategy B
### (Withdraw $15,700 from Bucket 1 until age 75)

Bucket 1 assets at 74 (end): $253,000
Bucket 2 assets at 74 (end): $197,000

RMD (Bucket 1) at 75: $9,878
Bucket 2 withdrawal at 75: $15,122

**Taxes owed 65-74: $0**
**Taxes owed at 75: $0**
**Taxes owed (cumulative) to age 80: $0**
**Taxes owed (cumulative) to age 90: $2,521**

Aaron doesn't need much help. His taxes are pretty low even using Strategy A. Nevertheless, if we run Strategy B at $15,700/year (Aaron's standard deduction) he can pay no taxes by age 80 and only $2,521 by age 90. Aaron cuts his taxes by more than 75 percent and has about $9,000 more left in Bucket 1 at age 90 (which increases from $38,809 to $47,437 in today's dollars). Aaron may not want to ignore the benefits of Strategy B.

Let's go right to Aaron 3.0, adding Social Security, other income, 3 percent/year account appreciation over inflation, and increasing his target income accordingly:

## Aaron 3.0

**Social Security: $36,000/ year at age 70**
**Dividends/interest/other income: $5,000/year**
**Target income: $60,000/year**
**3 percent annual post-inflation appreciation rate**

If Aaron uses Strategy A, he will see cumulative taxes at age 80 of $27,957 and by age 90 of $70,005. Taxes are a bigger issue for Aaron 3.0 than for Aaron 1.0. Taxes under Strategy A and savings at various withdrawal amounts for Strategy B are shown in the table below:

## Aaron 3.0

|  | Taxes owed by 80 | Taxes owed by 90 |
|---|---|---|
| **Strategy A** | $27,957 | $70,005 |
| **Strategy B** | | |
| $10,000/year | $18,513 | $54,734 |
| $15,000/year | $22,326 | $51,884 |
| $20,000 | $26,979 | $49,874 |
| $25,000/year | $32,190 | $48,421 |
| **$35,000/year** | **$47,796** | **$52,050** |
| $45,000/year | $67,408 | $67,408 |

Some savings arise both at age 80 and age 90 with the $10,000 withdrawal rate. When Aaron uses Strategy B at a $25,000 withdrawal rate, the news is better long-term. He has to pay more taxes by age 80—about $4,000 more. By age 90 he saves over $20,000, however, significantly more than the savings using a $10,000 withdrawal rate. Strategy B at $25,000 reduces his estimated taxes by about 30 percent. Strategy B works for single Aaron very well if he is patient, and even better if tax rates increase in future years. The $25,000 rate also means Aaron will transfer money from Bucket 1 to Bucket 2 after Social Security starts at 70 and before RMDs begin at 75—ideally, into a Roth account to grow and distribute tax-free.

Aaron will have $150,463 left in Bucket 1 and $166,632 in Bucket 2 (today's dollars) using Strategy B at $25,000/year. This compares with $291,501 in Bucket 1 but only $14,341 in Bucket 2 using Strategy A. Aaron will have more money left over at age 90, and *much* more tax-advantaged money, using Strategy B.

Now let's meet Ava. Let's go right to version 3.0 for Ava.

## Ava 3.0

**Bucket 1 account balance at retirement: $1.2 million**
**Bucket 2 account balance at retirement: $600,000**
**Retirement Age: 65**
**Social Security: $36,000 by age 70**
**Other income: $15,000/year**
**Target annual income: $120,000/year**
**3 percent annual post-inflation appreciation rate**

Let's get right to the results for Ava under each strategy:

|  | Taxes owed by 80 | Taxes owed by 90 |
|---|---|---|
| **Strategy A** | $208,213 | $433,687 |
| **Strategy B** | | |
| $35,000/year | $168,493 | $393,966 |
| $75,000/year | $203,917 | $342,351 |
| $115,000/year | $264,348 | $304,183 |
| $135,000/year | $298,908 | $312,090 |

Strategy B provides interesting options. At $35,000, Ava lowers her Taxes owed by both age 80 and age 90. The savings are about $40,000 at both age 80 and age 90, indicating that little further savings accrue after 80.

At a withdrawal rate almost equal to the target income, $115,000, the savings by age 90 are much greater: $129,504. However, this later savings comes at an earlier cost: By age 80 taxes total about $56,000 more at this withdrawal rate than under Strategy A. Strategy B at $115,000/year leaves $158,181 in Bucket 1 and $102,693 (today's dollars) in Bucket 2 at age 90. This is more money, and more tax-advantaged money, than Strategy A, which leaves just $184,564 in Bucket 1 and $0 in Bucket 2 at age 90. Strategy B is interesting as well because in the pre-RMD years the already-taxed Bucket 2 account receives the surplus withdrawals from Bucket 1 for use in future years. As discussed throughout the book, in this situation you are well served considering converting such excess tax-deferred withdrawals in a Roth account, where they grow tax-free and all gains stay tax-free on withdrawal.

Let's try one more singles scenario, this time with a more modest account:

### Trey 3.0

**Bucket 1 account balance at retirement: $300,000**
**Bucket 2 account balance at retirement: $200,000**
**Social Security: $30,000/year at age 70**
**Other income: $10,000/year**
**Retirement Age: 65**
**Target annual income: $50,000/year**
**3 percent annual appreciation rate**

|  | Taxes owed by 80 | Taxes owed by 90 |
|---|---|---|
| **Strategy A** | $22,657 | $59,973 |
| **Strategy B** | | |
| $15,000/year | $25,938 | $48,369 |
| $20,000/year | $31,073 | $48,840 |

Trey will pay about $25,000 in taxes by age 80 and about $60,000 by age 90 under the Conventional Wisdom strategy—which is modest compared to many of our other examples. But for Trey, those still add up to a sizable portion of his assets.

Fortunately, we have good news for Trey. Strategy B at a $20,000/year withdrawal rate can reduce his tax liability by age 90, with savings of about $13,000 or 22 percent. Similar to our examples involving larger asset bases, this strategy is best executed by transferring excess distributions (which will arise once Social Security starts) from the Bucket 1 accounts in the pre-RMD years to a Roth IRA.

These examples for our single friends confirm the same findings we made for our couple friends—Strategy B can save significant taxes in many scenarios. We kept this section shorter than our couples discussion, not out of any disrespect for single filers, but to expedite our progress to the most pressing issue of the day—how *you* can implement a strategy that can save *you* on taxes in retirement.

# Chapter Nine

## Let's Do it! Turn Your Chosen Strategy into a Tax-smart Withdrawal Plan Right Now—and Why You Shouldn't Wait

If you made it this far (or you like to eat dessert first and skipped the prior chapters to get to this one), you are ready to test your retirement accounts using Strategies A and B.

Let's start saving!

### Keep it Simple, Saver.

Everybody's situation is different. It is impossible to guarantee a strategy that is the perfect one. In any event, there are no guarantees here. Could we run through fifty different approaches and still not know whether a different strategy could save an additional $100 per year in taxes? Could the numbers vary from the estimates based on actual inflation rate, tax rates, and investment performance? Of course.

The good news: The withdrawal strategy is not based on particular numbers, but rather on a principle. That principle is that people waste the opportunity to use lower tax brackets before their RMD age when they use Conventional Wisdom withdrawal strategies, but seize the opportunity presented by those lower tax brackets when they use Strategy B. So long as the IRS charges taxes using the tax bracket approach—a pretty safe bet for the near future and then some—the principle will mean you will save taxes when you pick the right Bucket 1 withdrawal rate before your RMD age. We do not have to allow a fear of imperfection to stop us from implementing a strategy for withdrawals that could be a lot better than the one you were likely to use. We can keep it simple and still come out way better than we would have.

That's why we focused on just one simple, easy-to-implement withdrawal strategy. By illustrating one simple option, we can avoid information overload (also known as TMI) and pick a strategy likely to save taxes. The approach is simple enough—withdraw a target rate from your Bucket 1 IRA/401(k) accounts every year before your RMD age—that Savvy Savers can implement it in a few straightforward steps, using their existing accounts and investments.

Now for the fun part: let's pick your withdrawal strategy in three steps:

1. Input your financial information into the Retirement Tax Saver system.

2. Get the totals for taxes by age 80 and age 90 for Strategy A and Strategy B at various target withdrawals from Bucket 1.

3. Pick the Strategy B target withdrawal amount you like the best.

### Step 1: Input your financial information into the Retirement Tax Saver system.

First, gather the information you will need to input into the Retirement Tax Saver system. This includes:

1. **Your retirement age** (if you've already retired this will be your current age). This one is easy. The calculator assumes the earliest retirement age of 60. If you are or will retire at an age younger than 60, try running the Saver at age 60 and estimate your assets at that point.

2. **The age Social Security payments will begin** (if it's already started put your current age). This is a choice you need to make if you haven't already. Many tools exist to assist you in making this decision including the Social Security Administration website at https://www.ssa.gov/benefits/retirement/learn.html. For Savvy Savers in good health, I lean toward waiting until age 70 to take advantage of the 8 percent/year increase in benefits that could help if you live longer than expected. Most Savvy Savers who live shorter than expected won't run out of money even if Social Security is deferred. But the decision is yours—anywhere between age 62 and 70 is permitted for a starting age, absent exceptional circumstances.

3. **Your annual Social Security distribution in the first year.** If you are already collecting, just enter the amount you currently get annually and your current age. If you have not started yet and do not know this number, go to the Social Security website https://www.ssa.gov/myaccount/ (create an account if you haven't used this website before). It will provide a default monthly benefit at your full retirement age. If you select a different retirement age, it will let you pick an age between 62 and 70 and provide the monthly benefit at that age. Multiply that monthly number by 12, and that is the annual number to use.

4. If you get or will get a taxable **pension**, you will need the **year it begins**, and the **annual distribution amount** the year it begins. If you have already begun receiving checks,

use the current year and current annual distribution. Distributions are probably taxable, but you can contact your pension's administrator to find out for sure. At this stage, the calculator does not distinguish between pensions that include a cost-of-living adjustment and those that do not. If your pension does not include such an adjustment, the calculator will effectively overstate your pension in future years—although the calculator may be modified in time.

Note: If you receive or will receive **other fixed-amount taxable distributions, such as a fixed annuity**, include that annual distribution in the pension box (#4 above). If you have no other pension income, indicate the year the fixed annuity payments begin as the starting year. If you have pension income and the start date is the same or near the same as for the fixed annuity payments, you can use the same year. If one or the other of the pension or annuity fixed payments start much earlier, than you might consider including the fixed payments from the earliest one in the "other income" category (#5 below). This will necessarily be an approximation, but the Tax Saver system is frequently updated and may have a way soon to separately enter this information.

5. If you have **other taxable income**, such as dividends or interest, or a side job, include an annual amount for the aggregate of all of these taxable income sources. This number varies, so put in a fair approximation (for example, something accurate at least for the current year and/or the following year). Last year's tax return might provide good guidance.

6. **Assumed growth rate**. The system will default to an assumed after-inflation appreciation rate of 3 percent/year on your retirement accounts, which shows up as 1.03. If you want to assume no appreciation, enter 1.0. If you want

a different rate, enter that rate plus 1.0. For example, for a 5 percent appreciation rate, enter 1.05.

Gather the **balances of all the accounts** you will use for retirement withdrawals. You will need to add up all the account values that belong in Bucket 1 (tax-deferred) to get a total for that bucket and do the same for Bucket 2 (already-taxed accounts including "regular" accounts and Roth accounts).

7. **Bucket 1** ("401(k)" for short) includes the value of only the accounts that will be taxed when the money is withdrawn. It includes:

- Regular (non-Roth) IRA account values

- Regular (non-Roth) 401(k) account values

- The account value of tax-deferred annuities that are variable— in other words, accounts that do not pay and will not pay a fixed monthly amount. This goes in Bucket 1 if it will be taxed on withdrawal, and Bucket 2 if it will not be taxed on withdrawal. If your annuity provides fixed monthly or other periodic payments, we will deal with those separately (see below).

- Other accounts such as Keoghs, Simplified Employee Pension (SEP), and any other account that will be taxed when the funds are withdrawn.

Some accounts, including some IRAs, have a blend of taxable (tax-deferred) and nontaxable distributions. The Tax Saver system does not calculate the split for you. You can either pick the single bucket that most closely matches your account or subdivide the account into two accounts that represent the taxable and nontaxable portions and place the taxable portion in Bucket 1. For example, if you have a variable annuity worth $100,000 and it includes 20 percent or $20,000 in your after-tax contributions which will not be taxed on withdrawal, you can approximate this by inputting 80 percent or $80,000 into Bucket 1 and the other $20,000 into Bucket 2.

8. **Bucket 2** (already-taxed, after-tax, or "AT") includes the accounts that will not be taxed as income, or are taxed in a minor way, when the withdrawals are made. It includes:

- Investment accounts such as stock, mutual funds, or ETFs that are not in Bucket 1 accounts (although capital gains in these accounts are taxed at different, lower rates than income when the gains are realized).

- Checking, money market, and savings accounts that will be used in retirement.

- Untaxed portions of accounts that are partially tax-deferred such as variable annuities (see above for guidance on how to deal with such hybrid accounts).

- Roth 401(k)s and Roth IRAs also go into Bucket 2, because like the other accounts in Bucket 2 they are not taxed on withdrawal.

Unfortunately, some if not all of these numbers are hard to predict in the future, and the Tax Saver does not allow you to vary the amounts in future years anyway. You will need to use your best estimate. I would recommend you use your best estimate for the current year and one or two years into the near future, as these amounts can always be adjusted in later years based on your then-current situation.

110

9. **Your desired annual income**. You can use other web-based products to estimate the annual income you can draw based on your account values. If the income is so high that it depletes your accounts before age 90, then you may be too optimistic. The Tax Saver runs its simulation through age 90.

Rule of thumb: Multiply your retirement account values when retirement starts by 4 percent and add that amount to the annual sources of income including Social Security, pension, annuity, and other. This number will equal a reasonable annual target income amount in the Tax Saver calculator.

You should pace your withdrawals so that your money will last long enough in retirement. "The 4% rule is a common rule of thumb in retirement planning to help you avoid running out of money in retirement. It states you can comfortably withdraw 4% of your savings in your first year of retirement and adjust that amount for inflation every subsequent year without risking running out of money for at least 30 years."[32] Some suggest the approach provides too little in the early retirement years and more than necessary in later years when retirees may be less active and spend less. Nevertheless the 4% rule is simple and easy to follow.[33]

For example, if your account values total $800,000 and you will collect $30,000 in Social Security and $5,000 in interest, dividends, and other income, a suitable number to use for your annual (pretax) income may be around $32,000 (4 percent of $800,000) + $30,000 + $5,000 = $67,000. Round this number down to $65,000 and you should be fine with each strategy—in other words, the projected assets will not run out before you reach age 90.

---

32 Christy Bieber, "What is the 4% rule?" *Motley Fool*, Updated Dec. 8, 2021, https://www.fool.com/retirement/strategies/withdrawal/4-percent-rule/.

33 *Id.*

If some income sources will not start for several years, or if you are more conservative, you might want to adjust the target income down to avoid depleting your accounts too quickly before those sources kick in.

### *Step 2: Run Strategies A and B Using Your Numbers in the Tax Saver System*

Now for the most fun part of all. Go to www. retirementtaxsaver.com. There you will see a chance to log in (just register your name and email address to get on our list of updates on the Tax Saver system, updates on this book, and related information). After you log in, you will be prompted to input all of the information gathered in categories 1-9 as listed above. Note: the Saver device may make some changes over time to the categories listed here, so be sure to follow the directions on the website if they differ from the information here.

The system will automatically show you Taxes owed by 80 and Taxes owed by 90 for your information using Strategy A. That's the baseline, Conventional Wisdom scenario—the one we are trying to beat. Write that one down.

The system will then prompt you to try Strategy B. Which withdrawal rates should you look at for Strategy B? Feel free to try several different withdrawal amounts— that's part of the fun. As we showed for our example couples, the break points for tax brackets (see below) seem to have good karma for starting withdrawal rates to try out. Then you can see if you can beat them.

Depending on when you use the Saver, the tax brackets may be updated. As of 2023 here were the break points to consider for couples over 65:

| | |
|---|---|
| Standard deduction: | $30,700 |
| 10% bracket: add $22,000 = | $52,700 |
| 12% bracket add $67,450 = | $120,150 |
| 22% bracket add $101,300 = | $221,450 |
| 24% bracket add $173,450 = | $394,900 |
| 32% bracket add $98,300 = | $493,200 |
| 35% bracket add $231,250 = | $724,450 |
| 37% bracket | above $724,450 |

The first three break points ($30,700, $52,700, and $120,150) are the primary ones used in our examples throughout this book.

Try these bracket-based withdrawal amounts using Strategy B and note the tax savings by age 80 and age 90 for the best options versus Strategy A. Once you have those numbers noted, try some other withdrawal numbers higher or lower to see if you can "beat the break points." As you try different Strategy B withdrawal rates, write down the tax savings by age 80 and age 90 for each one to track which one will be the best for you.

### Step Three: Withdraw from Your Tax-deferred Accounts Based on Your favorite Strategy

Once you have identified your favorite Strategy B withdrawal rate, great. But no matter how much of an improvement the Retirement Tax Saver shows you will get, you won't get *any* benefit if you don't *use* the information you learn. Fortunately, you can implement the withdrawal strategy immediately.

How? Let's pretend we are Juan and Maria. Remember their situation? Here is a refresher:

## Juan and Maria

> **Bucket 1 account balance at retirement: $500,000**
> **Bucket 2 account balance at retirement: $300,000**
> **Social Security: $30,000/year at age 70**
> **Other income: $10,000/year**
> **Retirement Ages: 65**
> **Target annual income: $70,000/year**
> **Inflation multiplier: 1.03 (3 percent/year)**

We found Strategy B at $30,000 was a good option for Juan and Maria. To implement Strategy B, all Juan and Maria have to do is contact the firm that holds their tax-deferred 401(k) and IRA accounts. If they are 65 years old, they have not started Social Security in this scenario, and have not yet withdrawn any money from their 401(k) or IRA accounts. Assuming they have not yet withdrawn anything from those accounts in the current year, they may set up a one-time or monthly withdrawal plan that results in withdrawing $30,000 from those accounts this year.

If it is January, that's pretty easy and comfortable. Juan and Maria can withdraw $30,000/12 or $2,500 each month for twelve months from Bucket 1 and use the proceeds to live on, or, if anything is left over, to deposit in Bucket 2. And, of course, lower their taxes in future years.

But what if it is November? Is it too late for this year? No. Juan and Maria should not *spend* $30,000 of their $70,000 targeted annual income in one or two months, of course. But they can still *withdraw* $30,000 from the IRA/401(k) tax-deferred accounts before the end of the year. They can live off of part of that money and move the rest into one of their already-taxed accounts, like savings. They can even move the excess over to a Roth IRA provided they meet certain requirements (which we will not address in this book). Juan and Maria can also schedule (or make a note on their planner to schedule) automatic monthly withdrawals from their Bucket 1 accounts of $2,500/month the following year.

As this example shows, you can start implementing Strategy B late in the year. You don't have to *spend* all of your target Strategy B annual withdrawal just because you *withdraw* it from your Bucket 1 401(k) or IRA account. There is no reason not to take advantage of the lower tax brackets still available to you *this* year. If, as we assume, you are at least 65 and have $10,000 in other taxable income, withdrawing an additional $30,000 in taxable income will include $18,700 in tax-free money, and the remaining $11,300 taxed at 10%.

You'll need to use one of your sources to cover the taxes, knowing you're likely to save more in future years than what you pay this year. Depending on the time of year and other factors such as whether you have capital losses or your deductions exceed the standard deduction, you may need to have taxes withheld, or pay estimated taxes on the withdrawal(s). You won't need as much money from your Bucket 2 accounts to meet income needs, so it should be no problem covering the taxes from Bucket 2—which is good, because that withdrawal will not trigger additional income taxes.

Once you take the withdrawal from your Bucket 1 accounts, you have already started implementing the strategy. Good for you! I hope it was easy for you.

If it is November, you may ask, sure, I *could* implement the strategy this year, but what's the rush? Let's look at an extra reason *not to wait* even if it is December.

### *Congratulations, Younger Baby Boomer Savers—you may be able to save more*

Our analysis has focused on those who have yet to reach RMD but are nearing retirement or just retired. That is mainly because that group has control over pre-RMD age withdrawals from tax-deferred accounts. Add the other criteria of this book to the age range—namely, that you have been a Savvy Saver with substantial savings in both 401(k)/IRA tax-deferred accounts and already-taxed accounts and have at least a few years to go before you hit RMD age—and you have a group which I call the Younger Baby Boomer Savers. Why? Because they are Savvy Savers and they are born at the end of the baby boomer generation. They are younger than other baby boomers, but they are baby boomers, and they are savers—Younger Baby Boomer Savers. Plus, it is fun to say quickly—much easier than (and not to be confused with) the classic "rubber baby buggy bumpers."

Younger Baby Boomer Savers are the biggest beneficiaries of the strategies outlined in this book. Why? They can take *maximum advantage* of the few short years between now and 2026 to withdraw more from their 401(k)/IRA accounts using today's historically-low tax rates, and in the process lower their 401(k)/IRA account's exposure to higher rates after 2025.

You will be under the age of 72 when 2026 rolls around if you have a birthday after 1953. If you will retire before 2026 and want to use Bucket 1 without penalty, you probably have a birthday before 1966. This thirteen-year window, from 1953 to 1966, corresponds to the middle and end of the baby boomer generation (give or take a few Generation Xers). If your birthday falls within this window, this is your lucky day. Within this window, the younger you are, the more you should be able to benefit from implementing a retirement withdrawal strategy because you will be able to withdraw more years before RMDs begin.

For all these reasons, your withdrawal decision can have an outsized impact on taxes owed in retirement **right now** and over the next several years. That is because right now, federal income taxes are about as low as they have ever been, and because there is a good chance that rates will go up at some point. That **only makes Strategy B even better**—because it takes bigger taxable withdrawals sooner, *before tax rates go up*, and will save more taxes later.

There are only a handful of years between now and 2026 (depending on when you read this, maybe not even a whole handful). Each year you do *not* implement a withdrawal strategy like Strategy B will result in paying higher taxes in the future. Remember the discussion about "use it or lose it?" Well, once January 1 hits, if you haven't already "used" or taken a withdrawal from your 401(k) or IRA account, you've "lost" your chance to do so for that year's taxes. You can't get that back. Sure, consult with whatever financial or tax advisors you have. But don't wait until January 1— do it in time to take the withdrawal this year, if that is what makes sense for you.

If you follow these three steps, you are off and running to saving taxes by age 80 and/or age 90. Pat yourself on the back. Well done. But to get the most out of this strategy, read the next chapter about annual maintenance.

# Chapter Ten

## Review, Revise, Retain: Using Annual Checkups to Keep Your Plan Running Well and Save Even More

### *Annual Maintenance Plan: Keeping the Plan Up-to-Date— and Simple*

Just as a car needs an oil change regularly, your withdrawal strategy should be revisited at least once a year. Fortunately, it is easy with the Retirement Tax Saver system. "The advantage of owning a tax-diversified mix of assets once you reach retirement is that it helps you manage your tax burden on a year-to-year basis, per your circumstances."[34]

Rerun the calculator early in the fourth quarter of each year (e.g., in October) based on your then-current account balances, income needed for the remainder of the year, and other values. If you have $5,000 higher income because you took on a one-time consulting project or had more dividend and taxable interest payments than expected, consider reducing your year-end Bucket 1 withdrawals in a corresponding amount. If that source of additional income is not expected to recur, that may be enough to fine-tune your plan for year end. Alternatively, if you expect higher or lower income from any of your sources on

---

34  Larry Fox, "Consider taxes in your retirement savings strategy."

an ongoing basis, you may want to try running a few options again based on the updated numbers, and choose an updated amount to withdraw from Bucket 1 under Strategy B.

Some accounts may have performed better or worse than others—rerunning the numbers will maintain a tax-efficient strategy customized for your *current* situation, not the past. Tax rates may have changed. Rate changes that are incorporated into the Tax Saver system will be noted on the website www. retirementtaxsaver.com.

For fine-tuning, you also may want to adjust the strategy when you are on the cusp between tax brackets. Keeping the total taxable income just under the next tax bracket break point is a little extra insurance that what you take out now will be taxed at a lower rate than it would have been taxed at later. Also, because the standard deduction and tax brackets change with inflation every year, you will want to adjust your withdrawals accordingly. In fact, the Retirement Tax Saver assumes you will "keep up" in future years with the changes in brackets.

You also might be in a position to use itemized deductions that give you a bigger 0% tax bracket than the standard deduction. For example, if you make charitable contributions and have large interest payments on your mortgage and other deductions, you may have itemized deductions totaling $40,000, for example. If that is the case, consider increasing your 401(k)/IRA withdrawal accordingly. In other words, with a deduction that is $40,000 - $30,700 = $9,300 larger, take $9,300 more from a tax-deferred account. At a minimum, if you haven't started taking Social Security yet, make sure your taxable income totals at least your itemized deduction total to take full advantage of the 0% bucket. That is a no-brainer.

If you *have* begun Social Security, you may want to check to see if increasing your taxable income total in view of a higher deduction may move you above either of the provisional income thresholds for taxing Social Security—$32,000 for taxing 50 percent of Social Security, and $44,000 for taxing 85 percent of

Social Security (married filing jointly; the single filer thresholds are $25,000 and $34,000). That might be a reason to keep taxable income lower even if it does not use up the entire 0% tax bracket in view of your deduction. Remember, provisional income is approximately half of your Social Security income for the year plus your taxable income.

## Other Thoughts

Here are a few extra considerations.

**When to start Social Security.** If you haven't started Social Security yet, you may have choices as to what year you start. You can claim early and at a reduced payout at 62, at full retirement age (at 67 or another age depending on your birth year), or wait until 70. Each year you wait, the annual benefit increases about 7 percent per year until 67, then 8 percent from 67 to 70 (if you were born after 1942).[35] There may be good reasons apart from taxes for preferring one starting age over another, including health considerations. Taxes may be one consideration but may not be the dominant one.

As discussed above, Social Security may be taxed in part based on provisional income. That might be a reason to defer starting it. Deferral will allow you more years to take advantage of lower tax brackets for withdrawals from Bucket 1 without those withdrawals triggering an offsetting increase in taxes. But the interplay among all the income sources does not necessarily mean you should defer Social Security to reduce taxes. You can run the calculator with different Social Security starting ages and the corresponding monthly benefits and see how that choice affects taxes.

---

35  Social Security Administration, *Retirement Benefits,* 2021, *https://www. ssa.gov/pubs/EN-05-10035.pdf* at p. 4.

**Other income.** Adjust for more or less additional income such as assumed interest and dividend income. You may want to adjust your 401(k)/IRA withdrawal lower if your interest and dividend taxable income is higher than you expected, or you had unexpected income from another source. Or consider increasing the 401(k)/IRA withdrawal if those income sources are lower than expected.

**One-time events.** Are you looking for the right time to cash in U.S. Savings Bonds? Most people choose to pay taxes on the accumulated interest when they redeem their bonds. Or sell highly appreciated securities? If there is a significant tax event coming up and you can control when it happens, you may want to pick a year when you are in a lower tax bracket, when you have more itemized deductions, or when the additional interest added to income will not put you in a higher tax bracket. You can scale back 401(k)/IRA withdrawals if some other tax events will trigger an unexpectedly higher bracket this year. This is a good discussion to have with a financial or tax advisor.

### Beware of Kicker Taxes

This book is not meant to cover all tax issues. But it is noteworthy that some taxes arise or change depending on your income. If you can modify your withdrawal strategy to keep (for example) adjusted gross income under these thresholds but still withdraw the money you need, it could save you even more.

For example, long-term capital gains taxes are affected by taxable income. For 2023, the 0% rate applies for those with taxable income up to $44,625 (single) and $89,250 (married filing jointly). A 20% rate starts when income exceeds $492,300 (single) and $553,850 (MFJ). A 15% rate applies when income is between the 0% and 20% threshold.[36] Keeping your taxable income just under these thresholds could save a lot in capital gains taxes, if you have capital gains in that same year.

Using the strategies outlined in this book will help you manage capital gains taxes as well as income taxes; for example, if Strategy A would lead to taxable income after age 72 exceeding the 15% threshold for a married couple filing jointly, but Strategy B would keep taxable income below the threshold. That could lead to substantial savings on capital gains taxes. If using Strategy B causes taxable income before age 72 to exceed the 15% threshold, then deferring capital gains so that they generate taxable events in later years when taxable income is under the threshold might be an effective strategy. Also consider reducing the Bucket 1 withdrawals in a year with large capital gains to manage taxable income below the threshold. This could save, for example, $1,500 in taxes in a year with $10,000 in capital gains.

The Affordable Care Act also added a 3.8% Medicare surtax on net investment income. The tax applies to interest, dividends, and capital gains if modified adjustable gross income (MAGI) exceeds $200,000 (single) and $250,000 (MFJ).[37]

Important note: taxable distributions from IRAs and 401(k) s are not directly subject to the Medicare tax, but are included in determining whether your modified AGI is above the threshold for triggering the higher tax rate.[38] So if a distribution pushes

---

36  Rocky Mengle, "The 2022 Capital Gains Tax Rate Thresholds Are Out—What Rate Will You Pay?" Kiplinger, Nov. 10, 2021, https://www.kiplinger.com/taxes/capital-gains-tax/603735/2022-capital-gains-tax-rate-thresholds.

37  "The Medicare Surtax on Investment Income," www.investor.vanguard.com/taxes/medicare-surtax.

38  David Fisher, "How to Calculate Your Modified Adjusted Gross Income," TheBalance.com, updated Oct. 24, 2021, https://www.thebalance.com/how-to-calculate-your-modified-adjusted-gross-income-4047216.

you over $250,000, you will owe more taxes on dividends, capital gains, and interest.[39] If your planned IRA (Bucket 1) withdrawal was going to cause you to have $251,000 in MAGI, for example, and you are married-filing jointly and had significant investment income, consider reducing the Bucket 1 withdrawal to ensure MAGI stays below $250,000 for the year. That could save $380 on $10,000 in investment income. Or talk to a tax or financial advisor if you have one.

Consider bunching income in other years to stay below your threshold MAGI the year you will have higher investment income. Then you can forgo paying the extra 3.8% on the extra income.

Additional income in years beginning at age 63 may trigger higher monthly Medicare-related costs once you reach Medicare age. This is also a reason to consider delaying the start of Social Security payments.[40] The Medicare formula can create a surprise because it looks at MAGI two years *earlier* to calculate the *current* year's premium. For example, 2022 premiums are based on income in 2020. High MAGI in 2020 can increase Medicare premiums by hundreds or thousands of dollars in 2022, but there's nothing you can do from a planning standpoint in 2022 to change 2020 income. Moreover, this formula means income at ages 63 and 64 can affect your Medicare premiums in later

---

39   Michael Kitces, "How IRA Withdrawals In The Crossover Zone Can Trigger The 3.8% Medicare Surtax," Kitches.com, July 23, 2014, https://www.kitces.com/blog/how-ira-withdrawals-in-the-crossover-zone-can-trigger-the-3-8-medicare-surtax-on-net-investment-income/; and Sandra Block and Joy Taylor, "How 10 Types of Retirement Income Get Taxed," Kiplinger, Dec. 3, 2021, www.kiplinger.com/retirement/602231/how-10-types-of-retirement-income-get-taxed.

40   Carla Fried, "What you need to know about Medicare by age 63," The (Spokane, Wash.) Spokesman-Review, May 9, 2021, https://www.spokesman.com/stories/2021/may/09/carla-fried-what-you-need-to-know-about-medicare-b/.

years, before you even are eligible for Medicare (and probably before you were even thinking about paying for Medicare).

If you are younger than age 63, this formula might present an opportunity. If you could have MAGI above $200,000 in the year you turn 63 and thereafter, consider withdrawing more from Bucket 1 in the pre-63 years. Pre-63 withdrawals will not increase your Medicare premiums but may help you keep MAGI lower once you reach age 63, helping you to lower your Medicare Plan B premiums once you reach age 65.

For 2022, the lowest threshold for 2020 MAGI was $182,000 for a married couple filing jointly.[41] Monthly Medicare Part B premiums start at $170.10 for 2020 MAGI below $182,000. Premiums increase in five increments to $578.30 over more thresholds at $228,000, $284,000, $340,000, and $750,000.

Part B premiums are particularly hard to plan for because the government does not release the thresholds for a current year's income until two years later. Thresholds are adjusted annually for inflation, so you'd have to predict inflation in 2023 to know the 2022 MAGI thresholds that will apply to 2024 premiums.

### *Avoid Analysis Paralysis*

The above are examples of ways higher income can come back to bite you. The number of thresholds and traps for the unwary can make choosing a withdrawal overwhelming. Before you give up, however, keep a few things in mind. One, if you are below $80,000 in taxable income for the year, you have just one main concern: whether and how much your Social Security will be taxed. These other taxes generally aren't a concern.

---

41    Medicare.gov, "Part B costs," https://www.medicare.gov/your-medicare-costs/part-b-costs.

Two, if you will have between $80,000 to $250,000 in annual taxable income, your main additional concern is saving taxes on capital gains taxes if you are near $250,000 in taxable income.

Otherwise, the main headline is still that withdrawals now will lower your taxable income later. The tax bites will be less painful in future years if not avoided altogether if you find a way to make withdrawals in lower tax brackets for more of your early retirement years. Strategy B is likely to help you do that. Beware of these tax traps and trip-ups but understand that they are all the *more* reason to implement a withdrawal strategy with taxes in mind— not a reason to bury your head in the sand or throw in the towel on even trying to develop a strategy.

# Chapter Eleven

## Conclusion—Better Prepared for the Ride

If you picked your withdrawal strategy and executed a tax-smart income plan, congratulations! You have made the transition from Savvy Saver to Smart Spender. Don't forget to do a tune-up every year.

Maybe you are still mulling it over. There is a lot of information out there on retirement finances. Or perhaps you want to talk this over with your financial advisor. Or with Uncle Miltie, who understands this financial stuff well. Whatever the reason, that's fine if you want to take a pause—with one caveat addressed below. But before you go, let's at least recap what we learned.

1. Being a Savvy Saver in your preretirement years does not prepare you for withdrawals from your tax-deferred and other accounts once you start using the money you saved.

2. There are various penalties and restrictions for how you withdraw your money from your accounts in retirement that limit your options as a practical matter. Most notable is the 50 percent penalty for failing to take Required Minimum Distributions.

3. Even within the rules based on the restrictions and penalties, you have a lot of control over how much you take out of which account, and when, during retirement.

4. How you withdraw from your accounts—how much from each account and when—can significantly raise or lower your taxes over the course of your retirement.

5. The Conventional Wisdom approach to retirement withdrawals—waiting until RMDs start—can result in larger taxable distributions after RMDs begin in high tax brackets. That is Strategy A.

6. Strategy B, which begins fixed withdrawals from your tax-deferred accounts annually before RMDs begin (now between ages 73 and 75), can result in large tax savings by ages 80 and 90. Thousands, even tens of thousands of dollars, can be saved in many situations even for those holding retirement assets of under $1 million.

7. Strategy B can work better than Strategy A because it takes better advantage of lower tax brackets in the pre-RMD years. Those lower tax brackets can keep taxes down. Every year is a new opportunity to use or lose the lower brackets.

8. Different approaches, and different target withdrawal amounts, work for different people. Lots of people, however, will lower their taxes by implementing a withdrawal plan.

9. To pick a good target amount for Strategy B, it is useful to be mindful of the break points between changes in tax rates, starting with the standard deduction, which in effect is the maximum income for the 0% tax bracket.

10. You can go to www.retirementtaxsaver.com to run simulations for taxes owed based on Strategies A and B and your personal financial information. This will allow you to pick a strategy for yourself that will manage your taxes well in retirement.

11. Strategy B is easy to implement. It does not require any new investments or fees. It simply requires you to change how much you withdraw from your existing accounts.

12. Tax rates will rise in 2026 unless Congress affirmatively passes a law that changes them. Congress may raise tax rates before 2026 as well. All things being equal, taxable retirement withdrawals before 2026, or whenever tax rates rise, will be taxed at a lower rate than withdrawals in and after 2026.

13. The sweet spot for benefiting from implementing Strategy B for retirement withdrawals are Younger Baby Boomer Savers—those nearing or early in retirement in their fifties and sixties who are at least younger than 72. Those folks are best able to take taxable withdrawals from tax-deferred accounts in lower tax brackets before RMDs start and in doing so are best able to keep taxes down on post-RMD distributions.

14. You don't have to start at the beginning of the year to implement Strategy B to manage your taxes. As long as there is still time before December 31 to take or modify a withdrawal from a tax-deferred account, you can start this year.

15. To best utilize the strategies in this book, reevaluate your situation every year, perhaps around October, and adjust accordingly.

16. If you have a financial advisor or tax advisor, great. Talk to them about the strategies in this book. They should be able to help you pick a strategy that takes your entire financial situation into account and saves you taxes.

The caveat relates to points 13, 14, and 15 above. While it is fine to mull over these takeaways for a while, don't wait too long to decide. Every year that passes without implementing the strategies in this book is a wasted opportunity to manage taxes. And you can start this year, even if the year is almost over, to successfully begin implementing a beneficial strategy.

A final thought: Strategy B can also provide bridge income while you defer the start of Social Security. Deferring Social Security may make sense because benefits increase the longer you wait to start. The benefit increases 24% by waiting from age 67 to 70, for many people. That increase is for life. So saving on taxes is not the only reason to switch to Strategy B for retirement account withdrawals.

Whatever you decide to do, I hope you at least feel a little more prepared for the roller coaster ride as you shift from being a Savvy Saver to a Smart Spender.

Good luck!

# Disclaimers

This book is meant to be a source of information to assist you in making your own decisions about your finances. Laws and rules change, and many factors can come into play in specific situations that are beyond the scope of this book, which is intended to give general information that may relate to a wide variety of situations in different ways. The author and publisher do not represent or warrant the accuracy or completeness of this work or any related websites or materials and disclaim all express or implied warranties including without limitation warranties of fitness for a particular purpose. These materials could not be provided for your consideration as a practical matter, if doing so would result in the author and publisher undertaking any risk or liability of any kind.

The strategies and approaches discussed herein may not be suitable in specific situations. The publisher and author are not rendering legal, accounting, or financial advice or other professional services. If you seek personal professional assistance, seek professional tax and financial advice.

The publisher and author disclaim any liability, loss, or risk resulting from actions taken based on the information contained herein and are not liable for damages resulting from any such action.

Citations provided in this book are not intended to be endorsements of any organization or material provided or recommendations made. Nor should it imply that any cited organization or party endorses any of the statements or information contained herein.

Websites referred to herein may disappear or change or provide updates or modifications of the information provided herein.

Efforts were made to make the information in this book complete and accurate as well as useful, but there may be typographical as well as substantive errors. Moreover, many of the specific examples and calculations provided in this work are based on tax simulations prepared by the author using a confidential, patent-pending analytical tool. The tool is frequently modified and updated. It is not intended to be an indicator of actual taxes owed by any specific individual in any given year. Use the calculations and all other information contained herein at your own risk. The views and content expressed herein are solely the author's and not of any law firm or employer.

# Acknowledgements

With deep gratitude to:

Deb Englander for her wisdom and guidance throughout the publishing process. Tony Zeuli for his detailed review and thoughtful reflection on modifications, and for helpful feedback on the Retirement Tax Saver calculator. Don Trevarthen, Royce Schultz, Laura Moret, and Todd Obijeski for being the first to volunteer review a draft of the book, and for their helpful and encouraging feedback. John McDonald for his role as sounding board. Trevor McDonald for his instrumental role in developing the Retirement Tax Saver Calculator that revealed so many of the lessons in this book. McKenna Taylor for her design insights. Roshini Rajkumar for her "Wow" communication perspective. Darryl Strong for his inspiring and unbridled enthusiasm. My wife Kim for everything.

# About the Author

**Daniel McDonald** is a semi-retired intellectual property lawyer and creator of the retirementtaxsaver.com website. Dan has a B.S. in Electrical Engineering and a law degree, both from the University of Minnesota. Dan has been an attorney for over 36 years, admitted in Minnesota, Georgia, and various federal district courts, appellate courts, and the U.S. Supreme Court. He is also a registered patent agent authorized to practice before the U.S. Patent and Trademark Office. Recognized for many years as a SuperLawyer® and *U.S. News and World Report* Best Lawyer®, Dan has successfully presented and defended against dozens of multi-million-dollar patent, trademark and copyright claims. He has volunteered in many roles at the University of Minnesota including Chair of the Alumni Association, receiving the University's Alumni Service Award. Dan currently resides in Naples, Florida and enjoys bicycling, kick boxing, and traveling with his wife Kim.